Making Prayer Work

Other "Spiritual Companions"

Working with Angels
Celebrating Life
The Act of Meditation
The Way To Health
Healing Emotional Wounds
Defeating Evil and Sin
The Role Death Plays in Life
The Noble Mind & Its Uses
Finding Meaning in Life
The Connection
The Light of Initiation

Making Prayer Work

by Robert R. Leichtman, M.D. & Carl Japikse

ENTHEA PRESS
Atlanta, Georgia & Columbus, Ohio

This ebook edition was made possible by a gift to the Publications Fund of Light by Mark and Betty Peters

MAKING PRAYER WORK

Copyright © 1988 by Light

All Rights Reserved. No part of this book may be used or reproduced in any manner without written permission, except in the case of brief quotations embodied in articles and reviews. Printed in the United States of America. Direct inquiries to: Enthea Press, P. O. Box 251, Marble Hill, GA 30148.

ISBN 0-89804-828-1

Table of Contents

Introduction   6
Praying Effectively   7
Invoking Divine Life   67

Introduction

These essays on **Making Prayer Work** were first published as part of a set of 31 essays written by Robert R. Leichtman, M.D. and Carl Japikse on *The Life of Spirit.* They can also be found in Volume III of that series.

Making Prayer Work has been selected to be reprinted in this special gift edition because it is probably the clearest, most helpful explanation of prayer in print.

Father David Hoover, a Roman Catholic priest writes: "These essays are pure wisdom. They are universal and very practical. If ever there existed spiritual guidance for modern man, it is here."

The first essay deals with praying effectively; the second with invoking divine life.

Praying Effectively

Focused Devotion

Of all the tools of the life of spirit, prayer is the one most widely used to deepen our relationship with God. In fact, for many people it is the *only* means used to relate to God directly. And yet, even though almost everyone has prayed one time or another, and has an opinion about the efficacy of prayer and its role in life, most of us have only a vague concept of the full potential of prayer and how to pray effectively.

Most people would define prayer as the act of talking to God. Yet this is where agreement ends. For some, prayer is a formal ritual in which precise wording and phrasing are all important. For others, it is an act of pleading with the Creator to intercede and give support. And for all too many, it is just another joyless routine performed by rote—because it is expected of them.

None of these concepts of prayer touches its real power, however. As a result, when people pray, the effort is sometimes effective, sometimes not. Some people conclude that this is because God is whimsical—or because humans are sinful. But these are misleading conclusions. The sporadic effectiveness of our prayers is due to our own lack of skill in praying—not divine caprice or human unworthiness.

Our prayers *can* be effective. Prayer is meant to be one of the major tools for interacting with the life of spirit—for contacting divine forces and focusing them into our life, the lives of other people, or even the life of groups and nations. To raise our ability to pray to this level, however, we must do more than just believe in prayer. We must see prayer as an intelligent process that serves a definite purpose, and therefore adheres to specific principles. As we master these principles and learn to apply them in our thoughts, words, and deeds, our capacity to pray effectively flourishes.

What are the purposes and principles of prayer? Even though most people believe prayer is the act of talking to God, it is really something more. The concept of talking to God tends to emphasize the outer form and words of prayer too much. The real substance of a prayer is the *quality* of the thought, feeling, and intention with which we pray, not the *words* we choose. A prayer should increase our love for and responsiveness to some quality, ideal, or power of the life of spirit, because the purpose of prayer is to attune our mind and heart and will to divine life, so we can enrich our life with a higher quality or dimension of consciousness. We should therefore approach prayer as an act of *focused devotion,* because it is devotion which builds this love and responsiveness. As we focus our devotion on God and the life of spirit within us, we pray. The stronger our devotion, the more effective our prayer will be.

Lacking devotion, we cannot pray. We may form the words of standard prayers and speak them aloud, but we do not pray. We may form images of powerful visualizations, but we do not pray. Words are merely words, as images are merely images, unless we add the extra ingredient of focused devotion. It is devotion that makes a prayer a prayer.

Some express devotion as a strong faith in the love and concern of God for our needs as humans. Others experience devotion as adoration for the presence of God. But the most common way we touch devotion is by trusting in the strength and benevolence of divine forces, knowing they are responsive to our sincere requests and are able to help us confront our problems and resolve them.

The devotion which is the basis of all prayer is not just a pleasant mood. Feelings, no matter how well intentioned, tend to be focused on wishes and desires—on what we hope to receive. Our devotion, therefore, should be intelligently directed—an expression of our values, priorities, and understanding of life, not our feelings.

A prayer may include an expression of need, but it should always be much more than this alone. *It should focus us on spiritual forces.* It should lift us out of our need and open us to the belief and expectation that the power of God is close at hand and ready to work through us, if we but request it. Understanding this, we can readily grasp the major characteristics of effective prayer:

1. The intent of prayer is to make an appeal

to the life of spirit, the source of life—not to our subconscious wishes.

2. The proper motive of prayer is to bring something of heaven to earth—not just passively adore God.

3. Prayer *changes* us—our understanding, perspective, tolerance, or sense of grace. Prayer does not coerce God into performing a miracle on our behalf, but helps us increase our devotion to and ability to use some spiritual force or quality.

If we understand these three key characteristics, then it becomes relatively easy to determine what makes any given prayer effective. An effective prayer is one which lifts us out of our need, helps us become aware of our divine capacity to respond to this need, and opens up our own heart and mind and will so that we are responsive to working with this divine force. This enables us to meet our needs *spiritually.*

All of this, of course, can happen silently, without a single word or phrase being uttered. In most cases, however, the inner attitude of focused devotion will take shape as words and perhaps even images, leading to a verbalized statement of our prayer. Nevertheless, it should be remembered that it is the essence of prayer—the focused devotion—which produces the results. The words and images we may associate with this devotion help us focus it, but *they are not the real prayer!*

The true essence and function of prayer become easier to understand by contrasting prayer with meditation, another of the tools of the life of spirit. Prayer and meditation are often confused with each other, because they are both used to bring elements of the life of spirit into the personality. But while prayer is a means for *appealing* to the heavenly realms of spirit for help in living at the physical level, meditation is the process of actually *visiting* heaven and acting from the spiritual level.

This may seem to be a trivial distinction, but it is really quite profound. It is far easier, after all, to call someone on the telephone than it is to travel the distance to visit him or her personally. Telephoning requires little effort or preparation, while traveling requires a good deal of both. And the contact which is made in person embraces the whole scope of our state of mind, appearance, and personal presence.

In the same way, prayer is a limited but highly focused effort to contact a specific quality of spirit and apply it to a well-defined need. Meditation is the effort to raise the whole of our consciousness into the realm of spirit for transformation, self-renewal, and redemption. To some extent, both prayer and meditation help us contact spirit and incorporate it into our life—all of the tools of spirit do. But each has its own special function.

The comparison with meditation also reveals something else quite important about prayer. Meditation becomes most effective once the love, wisdom, and will of spirit are able to control the process of meditating. But it is not the function of prayer to identify with spirit this extensively. In prayer, the personality initiates the contact and retains control of most aspects of the process. It is therefore a tool designed to be used by the personality to participate in the life of spirit while still involved in mundane activities.

This is the reason why prayer is the most universally recognized and used of all the tools of spirit. But it is also the reason why so many prayers are less than effective. The personality remains in control and can easily distort—and even pervert—the process of praying.

These distortions of prayer are far more common than most of us realize. In fact, some of them have become so common they have been accepted as "natural." Nevertheless, they are not in harmony with the purposes of spirit or the principles of effective prayer. In most cases, they are just projections of the unenlightened personality, which has an amazing capacity to see the world exclusively from the perspective of its own problems, prejudices, fears, and desires. The most prevalent distortions of prayer are:

Wishing instead of praying. When many people pray, they focus on the object of their prayer—their desires and wishes—rather than the divine powers and resources that could help them. As a result, their "prayers" become little more than exercises in fantasy fulfillment—not genuine interactions with spirit. It must be understood that God is not a great, supernatural Santa Claus who exists primarily to satisfy our whims and desires. Nor is prayer meant to be a tool for magically pulling miracles out of a hat. It is a way of connecting ourself with spiritual resources of help and support which we can then use in our conduct of life.

The idea of praying for "a miracle," however, is so deeply ingrained in our way of thinking that even people who understand the true significance of prayer often continue to pray as though every want and desire they entertain can command God to fulfill it. This is arrogance of the highest order. Of course, most of these requests are never fulfilled—and when they are, it is not God Who grants them. Selfish prayers can only be answered by selfish practices—by telepathically manipulating family, friends, and even aspects of the lower psychic planes to provide that which is desired. Such "praying," however, is really only "preying."

The biggest problem with wishing in the name of praying is that it gradually leads to a phenomenon which might be called "Godless positive thinking." We become so oriented to obtaining our selfish wishes and desires that we pay less and less attention to divine forces, until God drops entirely out of the picture. Our full devotion is focused on our fantasies. Obviously, such prayers will not be effective. And yet, when these prayers are not answered, the one who prays usually assumes the problem lies in his lack of faith—not in his lack of orientation to God.

Running through routines instead of praying. Some people pray because it is a duty which has been imposed on them by religious dogma. They are expected to pray, and so they do, in order to conform to these expectations. But they are praying only to a god of dogma, not a God who calls us into the benevolent presence of divine love. As a result, they go through the motions and words of their prayers but never cultivate the sense of faith, devotion, and trust which is the core of all effective prayer. Their prayers are joyless tasks, burdensome chores to be hurried through and forgotten. As such, they are ineffective. An effective prayer fills us with a quiet, pervasive sense of joy—the joy of knowing that we are communing with divine life, the source of our humanity, intelligence, creativity, and ability to express goodwill.

A related problem is that many people love short cuts—especially short cuts to the life of spirit. So religion has often emphasized the mechanical aspects of prayer to the exclusion of devotion. It has devised rosary beads to keep track of prayers and prayer wheels to repeat prayers automatically. It has set forth rules about praying with the eyes closed, knees bent, and hands clasped. Some of these rituals have merit, some do not. But all of them are a distraction when they divert our attention away from the real goal of prayer—to contact the inner forces of spirit. There are no short cuts in praying effectively.

Visualizing instead of praying. Visualization has become a very popular technique of the new age, with many people believing it to be the central skill of working with spirit. These people therefore assume that visualizing the object of their prayers is the most important—if not the only—part of praying.

Visualization is useful, but its significance has been vastly overrated, both in prayer and meditation. It is not actually a tool or a skill of the life of spirit, but an adjunct to it—a means of focusing the forces we contact in order to meet our needs. As always, the key to prayer is linking ourself with proper spiritual resources through devotion. If we fail to do this, no visualization, no matter how spectacular, will make our prayers effective.

Unfortunately, the process of prayer has been blurred by a number of very spiritual people who are excellent channels for divine forces and blessings. These people are in such close harmony with spirit that even a casual visualization does become a powerful focus and projection of spiritual energy. Carelessly, they have assumed that the power lies in the visualization, but it does not. It lies in their continuous devotion and rapport with spirit. People who lack this strong devotion are unable to achieve the same level of success. So it is important to realize that first we must build a strong base of devotion, and then add creative visualization.

Brooding on problems instead of praying. The personality has an innate tendency to dwell excessively on its problems. And it tends to carry this preoccupation with hardship into prayer. But this can diminish the value of our prayers, as too much attention to personal woes and inadequacies will prevent us from contacting the life of spirit—which is the whole point of praying. *Our potential for making things better can be driven out of our mind and heart if we permit ourself to become obsessed with our difficulties.*

It is understandable to be dragged down in

this way during a time of acute crisis. At such times, the willingness of friends to pray with us and help us rise above the immediacy of outer circumstances—and our own emotional reactions—is invaluable. Their assistance can help us find the presence of God once again. But some people are so bogged down in their problems and self-pity that they brood on them even when circumstances do not warrant it. This short circuits the potential of prayer.

Groveling instead of praying. When identification with problems and hardships becomes chronic, a person may begin to believe himself unworthy of God, which means, by default, that he weakens his capacity to conquer his problems. It also means he rejects help which might be offered to him, either from family and friends, or from the life of spirit. The potential of prayer is obscured by his guilt, self-condemnation, and feelings of inferiority—powerful barriers indeed.

It is sad that some religions actually encourage such inferiority, by teaching us to feel unworthy in the face of God. We all have our weaknesses and flaws, to be sure, but there is also a part of us that is noble and divine.

Anything which makes our weaknesses and flaws seem more important or greater than our nobility and divinity will also make prayer more difficult.

Fearing God instead of praying. In some cases, the sense of personal unworthiness is compounded by projecting it onto God, believing God to be a harsh, judgmental being we must fear, not love. Of course, this tendency is strongly reinforced by a good deal of misguided dogma and harsh, judgmental religious fanatics. But whatever the source, it renders prayer ineffective. It is not possible to enter into a devotional rapport with God—the object of prayer—while simultaneously fearing divine retribution. Once again, we are actually *rejecting* God.

The fear of God is a difficult problem to overcome, because we cannot just switch back and forth from fearing to loving God. The two states are mutually incompatible. To learn to pray effectively, therefore, we must leave behind us those people who still fear God and begin associating with those who have discovered that God is compassionate and benevolent and asks for our love, not our fear.

Almost every one of these distortions of prayer arises from the fact that the personality controls the process of prayer and subtly colors it to suit its own expectations and needs. It makes the act of prayer only a personal experience, and thereby limits its effectiveness. To the degree that we can rise above this personal bias, however, and learn to pray with a measure of detachment, we can overcome this limitation.

It may seem odd that the ideal attitude of prayer is an impersonal one, especially since so much has been written in recent times about the need for a "personal" relationship with God. All too often, however, the search for such a personal relationship has trivialized God, rather than ennobling us. The purpose of prayer is to lift us out of our personal, selfish ruts and attitudes and help us discover the real presence of spirit.

Once again, there is no substitute for focused devotion. If, as we pray, we devote our thoughts and feelings to the benevolent capacity of divine life to help and support us, this act will lift us out of our preoccupation with personal need and gradually lead us to a more spiritual, impersonal attitude toward life. It will help us break through our wishes and desires, the dogma and tradition we have been taught, and our worries and fears, so that we can discover the real presence of spirit. And once we discover this presence, even in small measure, our relationship with spirit will change dramatically. Instead of just "talking" with spirit, we will be able to *act* hand in hand with spirit, thereby tapping more and more of its creative power.

This is the value of learning to pray effectively.

Our Pathway To God

Many people think of prayers only in set ways, as petitions which begin by addressing God and conclude by intoning "Amen." In reality, there are many different types of prayer—and many different ways they can be used.

One of the most common types of prayer—the informal prayer—is in fact the least discussed. The informal prayer is a half-spoken or wholly unspoken prayer of the heart or mind—a steadfast yearning, a strong concern about someone, a sharply defined conviction about work to be done, or a firm dedication to doing the right thing. All of these *can* be prayers, if they are manifestations of sincere need and are sustained by a steady faith that God does help and support human activities.

Quite possibly the best description of the effectiveness of informal prayer was written not by a clergyman but by Mark Twain. In his classic short story, "Letter to the Earth," Twain writes in the manner of a recording angel reporting on the personal prayers of a wealthy but avaricious coal dealer, Abner Scofield. Since Scofield is a hypocritical man given to posing as a proper Christian but not acting as one, the recording angel automatically discounts all prayers he has said out loud. Instead, only "secret supplications of the heart" are counted. These are the silent desires and yearnings of his true character—almost all of which are destructive curses directly opposed to his "public prayers."

Of course, destructive curses and thoughts of malice and resentment are not prayers, because they do not connect us with the realm of spiritual force. But Twain's thesis is a penetrating and important one. The mainstream of our unspoken thoughts and attitudes is significant in determining our true state of consciousness and rapport with God. If our habitual level of thought and feeling is noble and benevolent, it becomes to some degree a prayer which activates opportunity and assistance in our life. But if our habitual level of thought and feeling is selfish, malicious, and crude, it smothers the life force of any prayer we might utter, making it ineffective. Unfortunately, the majority of people tend to be negative much of the time, making it difficult for them to pray effectively.

If we are going to pray effectively, therefore, we must make sure that we do not inadvertently generate destructive attitudes that will undermine our nobler intent. And we should also come to appreciate the power of *enlightened* thought and feeling—that a sincere aspiration to change something, a strong desire to be helpful, and a steadfast compassion for others are all potent prayers, even though we may never translate them into words. In fact, they often are far more powerful and effective than spoken prayers—certainly the spoken prayers of people who do not mean them.

This is not to imply, however, that we never need to be bothered with spoken prayers. Since prayer is one of the important ways we bring the abstract and universal forces of spirit into our world, anything which gives spirit a clearer and more precise focus will make the process more powerful. Verbalizing our prayers helps us in exactly this way, by shaping our convictions and attitudes into a specific form. It organizes our petitions and adds richness of detail to our prayers. This is true of the whole range of prayer, from simple blessings for the food we eat to complex prayers which are part of the formal liturgy of a worship service.

In using spoken prayers, however, we must take care not to be distracted by the words. This is especially true in prayers that we use over and over again, reciting from memory. It is all too easy to fall into a hypnotic trance in which we stop thinking about what we are saying. Instead, we must be sure to maintain a continuous state of focused devotion on the inner qualities and dimensions of spirit we are praying to. In this way, we can remain in harmony with the purpose of our prayer.

Just as there are many human needs, there

are also many types of prayer. Any attempt to list the variety of prayer will of necessity be somewhat arbitrary. But it is valuable to do so, because it helps illustrate the basis of effective prayer. The major types of prayer, both formal and informal, are:

Prayers of praise and blessing—the focusing of pure devotion on the divine potential in some aspect of life. Virtually anything can be blessed by prayer—our work, a relationship, other people, conditions in life, humanity as a whole, and other kingdoms of life. But praying in this way involves more than just generating and projecting a good feeling toward some aspect of life; that would just be a personal blessing. When we pray, we contact divine life—in this case, the capacity of the love of God to magnify the noble and divine potential in people and situations. A prayer of blessing, properly executed, lifts us out of our own opinions and feelings and aligns us with the nurturing force of divine love. As a result, it is possible to bless with a clear conscience not only those people and circumstances we approve of, but also those that are destructive and antagonistic to us. The blessing calls forth the divine forces which will neutralize and redeem the destructive and antagonistic tendencies. A good example of this type of prayer would be a blessing for our work:

May divine wisdom and love pour through my heart and mind to guide and sustain me as I seek to do my work.
May the light of God go before me to prepare my way, and may it strengthen my will to serve.
Let goodwill be the keynote of all I do.

The heart of this prayer is a strong devotion to expressing the light of God through the work we do. By requesting its assistance, we magnetically set in motion the psychological and spiritual energies which will draw to us the opportunities and conditions we need to express this light through our work. But the prayer also clearly states that this blessing will come through our own acts and intentions, not through some kind of magical intervention. The blessing will only bear fruit tangibly if we work to help it manifest in our own talents and activities.

Some people might think it would be easier

merely to say, "God bless my work," and be done with it. Brevity, however, is not always a virtue in prayer, unless we have a clear understanding and faith that this divine blessing will work directly and indirectly *through us* as its primary channel of manifestation. Our own orientation to spirit is crucial to praying effectively, and the more our spoken prayers can spell out this devotion and responsiveness, the more powerful they will be.

The same kind of prayer can be used to bless creative projects, religious institutions, our school system, the nation's economy, or even the welfare of the planet. Some might scoff at such grandiose applications of individual prayer—but only those who do not know how to pray effectively. Since it is not our personal blessing but rather a divine blessing we are praying for, such prayers can be enormously beneficial—especially when a large number of sincere people pray for the same blessing. A good example of this kind of prayer on an international level would be a blessing for peace:

May the love and peace of God be with all who suffer.

May divine intelligence and patience guide those who strive to be peacemakers.
And may goodwill be the keynote.

Once again, we could have simply prayed, "Blessed are the peacemakers." Said with sincere devotion to a God of peace and love, this would be an effective prayer. Yet the addition of a few more words blesses the cause of peace as well as those who strive to bring it, and states the qualities of consciousness which will truly resolve conflict and generate peace. In this way, it distinguishes between those who work intelligently to establish peace and those who claim to promote peace but only stir up trouble.

Prayers of cleansing and banishment—the focusing of divine authority and law to dispel negative energies or influences and enhance our divine potential. These prayers can be used to cleanse our consciousness, physical places, and even objects. In some cases, the prayer is focused more on enriching divine qualities than on banishing negative forces, but the result is the same. A good example of a prayer for cleansing our attitudes would be:

Mother-Father God, You have created us to be immortal and made us in the image of Your own power and life. Our heritage is wisdom, love, strength, and health, but our heart is restless until we find union with You.

Look with love upon us now, so we may be filled with the brightness of Your light and become an unspotted mirror of Your power, the image of Your goodness, both outwardly in our bodies and inwardly in our mind and heart.

Because this prayer clearly focuses our devotion and adoration on the creative source of life, it should be obvious that it is more effective than a simple declaration such as, "God, make me well!" It recognizes that there is a divine pattern that governs our well-being and seeks to contact this pattern, so it can be magnified and established in our own consciousness and health. It also spells out our direct involvement in the cleansing and healing we seek.

A more formal prayer could be specifically directed at banishing harmful influences as well as summoning positive, spiritual forces. It is not wise to use prayers of this type, however, unless we are able to remain steadfast in our faith that God is omnipotent and pervades all of creation with divine order. A trace of hesitation or show of fear will tend to diminish the effectiveness of the prayer. An example of this kind of prayer would be:

O God, the One Who has breathed divine life into our universe and is the continual source of its existence, bring forth Your power over this place (or object) and grant that every power of adversity and every illusion or artifice of evil be banished from it. May this place (or object) be filled with Your light and love, so it may promote health of body and mind. In the name of our God of love, so be it.

This is not just a prayer to fight what we think is evil; more importantly, it is an act of devotion to the love and ideal health of divine life. It recognizes the pervasiveness and authority of God and calls them forth to dominate the place or object in question, thereby leaving no room for evil or illusion.

Prayers for assistance and specific benefits—the focusing of divine guidance and support for ourself, another person, or a group. There is a great temptation in using this type of prayer, of course, to think only of our own desires, possessions, fears, envy, or prejudice, but succumbing to this temptation greatly reduces the effectiveness of the prayer. The tendency of some people to ignore divine will and assume that if God cares for them heaven will deliver what they ask for promptly and without grumbling is not a proper basis for this or any kind of prayer. It is therefore imperative that we approach prayers for assistance and specific benefits *impersonally*, letting the prayer lift us out of our need and focus us in the proper divine resources. A good way to do this is to make the prayer contingent upon divine wisdom. In other words, if what we are praying for is not in harmony with what is best for everyone involved, we ask that it be automatically corrected so that it is. Some may consider this amendment unnecessary, of course, but these people should reflect on the fact that not all things they have asked for and received in life have turned out to be as beneficial as they originally believed they would be.

A simple example of this kind of prayer would be: *God, help me be strong so I may complete our work.* Although brief and direct, the request is specific and indicates that we are responsive to a noble purpose, not selfish gain. It also clearly indicates that we expect to be the channel for this divine assistance. Other situations might require a more detailed prayer, however. A good example of a prayer for the healing of another person would be:

O Mother-Father God, You have made us in Your own image as an expression of Your love. We pray now for the healing and renewal of _____ in mind and body, insofar as this is possible. May he be lifted into Your light, so that his perfect pattern of health is energized and his body and personality are made whole.
For these blessings, we are deeply grateful.

The appeal of this prayer is directed at the divine source of all human life and form, asking for a personal transformation and redemption that will lead to the healing of mind and body. Yet this healing will conform to a divine pattern—not our personal expectations. Moreover, the prayer focuses entirely on the divine qualities needed for the healing, not on the distress or disability the object of our prayer is suffering. In this way, the tone of the prayer remains devotional from start to finish, thereby increasing its effectiveness.

Another example of a prayer for assistance is the well known Unity prayer for protection:

The light of God surrounds me.
The love of God enfolds me.
The power of God protects me.
The presence of God watches over me.
Wherever I am, God is.

This brief prayer, designed to attract divine forces to add strength, reassurance, and vitality to every level of our existence, has been a solace to many anxious and distressed people for many years. Presented in a strongly affirmative style, it implies a dedicated faith in and love for a benevolent God Who seeks to help all people. When said with a sincere devotion to God, it attracts spiritual forces which do serve to protect and support our well-being of body and mind.

Prayers of thankfulness and gratitude—the focusing of divine providence into our character and self-expression. Although the average person thinks of prayer mostly in terms of asking for something, the prayer of thankfulness is one of the most powerful in its capacity to transform and enrich our life. Its purpose is not just to thank God for the blessings and benefits we receive, but more importantly, to help us develop a constant habit of recognizing and responding to the providential nature of the life of spirit. Prayers of thankfulness help us become aware of the full richness of the interaction of spirit with the life of the personality. The habit of praying in this way teaches us that our sincere and genuine requests of spirit are answered—often in ways far greater than we originally imagined. An example of this kind of prayer would be a prayer of thankfulness for the opportunities we have received to prosper in our chosen career:

O Mother-Father God, Your divine abundance is a rich and fertile field in which we all labor. For the talent You have given me to develop and employ, I am grateful. For the many opportunities which have arisen allowing me to make a contribution to the well-being of humanity, I am thankful.

It can be especially powerful to use this

kind of prayer during times when we may be tempted to believe that we have no cause for thankfulness or gratitude. It orients us once again to the providence of divine life, so that we will be alert and responsive to the opportunities which do arise in our life.

Universal prayers—the focusing of divine benevolence for a variety of purposes and the good of all. Many of the best known and most revered prayers—the Lord's Prayer and some of the Psalms—are of this type. They affirm the presence of a God Who is benevolent and concerned with our human condition, and can be used to contact this divine presence no matter what our need may be. A simple example of this type of prayer would be:

O heavenly Mother-Father God, we are grateful for Your constant presence in our lives and homes, and for Your holy order and justice. May You continue to keep us in the protection of Your power. May divine light and love surround us and all people constantly. And may it be so.

Like all effective prayers, this one affirms the qualities we seek to contact and declares our devotion to them. It creates a spiritual atmosphere for all we do, so that our involvement in the life of spirit can be a universal experience, not just an occasional one.

Each of these types of prayer can be widely adapted to serve specific needs as they arise. As we pray, we should always keep in mind that the choice of words is important in helping us focus the qualities and forces we seek, but it is not the words which form the substance of our prayer. The substance of our prayer is always the focused devotion we direct at the life of spirit. The type of prayer we employ and the words we use to clothe our thoughts are the *channels* of this devotion.

At the same time, it is useful to understand that there is great value in the repeated use of traditional prayers as ritual. The accumulated devotion of millions of people using a similar prayer over hundreds or even thousands of years creates a potent force which benefits us all. Esoterically, it opens up a well-traveled path to heaven which makes it easier for the rest of us to follow.

Whether we use a standard prayer, however, or one that is an honest expression of our own thoughts and needs, the purpose of prayer is the same: to lift the personality out of its absorption in the mudane elements of life and enable it to contact the life of spirit.

And as we pray, we build our own pathway to God.

Interacting With Divine Life

As important as prayer is to the life of spirit, it is amazing how sloppy and careless some people are in their habits of prayer. In part, this is because religion has done a very poor job of teaching us the skills of effective prayer. But it is also due to the fact that we do not appreciate the full value and potential of intelligent prayer. We tend to view it one-dimensionally, as an opportunity to talk to God and present our needs, so God can take care of them for us. As a result, we often do not give much more thought to praying than we do to making a telephone call to a friend. In fact, many people think of praying in that way—as though it were a phone call to God. This is one of the reasons why so many prayers are ineffective.

For prayer to be a meaningful tool of spirit, we must give it far more importance than we give to an ordinary telephone call. At the very least, we should think of it as a call to someone extremely important. Because telephone calls are such a routine part of our life, we seldom take any time to prepare ourself before making one. The one exception is when we are calling someone of stature—our attorney, a physician, or perhaps a government official. Then we try to prepare ourself as best we can. We make sure we are alert, have sufficient time to finish the call, and have carefully thought through the topics we wish to discuss. In this way, we put ourself in a proper state of mind before dialing.

We must prepare for prayer in much the same way. In fact, the preparation ought to be more intense, because we are not actually dialing an important person, we are contacting God! God is available to be contacted—we will not get a busy signal—but we must make the contact on God's terms, not ours. The guidelines for contacting the life of spirit through prayer have already been determined by divine authority and wisdom. If we understand them and adhere to them, our prayer will be successful. But if we insist on making our own rules, it will generally fail. *It is our responsibility to adapt our thinking, feeling, and intention to become responsive to the life of spirit.* We cannot expect God to adapt to us.

In this regard, it is valuable to understand that the mechanism of prayer lies in our own consciousness. Whether or not we make contact with any aspect of the divine therefore depends wholly upon our own capacity to focus our consciousness correctly. For this reason, the preparation we must make in order to pray effectively goes far beyond just deciding what we need or want. We must focus our emotions in a state of aspiration and devotion to God, fill our thoughts with a powerful sense of trust in divine power, and fix our intentions on a steady dedication to making God a partner in our life. This may take more than just a few moments. Responsiveness to divine impulse is not a part of the ordinary state of mind for most people—even most people who believe in God. If we keep in mind, however, that the central feature of effective prayer is focused devotion, and practice attaining this kind of devotion on a regular basis, preparing to pray will become a comfortable and familiar habit.

Prayer itself can be a valuable aid in preparing our consciousness for prayer. The purpose of such prayer is to raise our psychological tone and consciousness to a higher level than before—a level where prayer can be more effective. A good example of using prayer to prepare ourself in this way would be:

O holy Creator of life, You are the source of love and inspiration to all. Your infinite peace and grace are constant blessings, even though my attention is often directed away from them by ordinary events.

I yearn to know and experience more of Your love and light, so that I may create a closer bond with You. I call on You now to enfold me in Your gentle power and love.

In this way, we declare our devotion to a God of love and establish our firm aspiration to achieve a meaningful contact with divine forces. If sincerely done, saying this prayer will focus our thoughts, feelings, and intentions properly while simultaneously drawing in divine qualities which will enrich our experience in praying.

There are, however, a number of subtle

attitudes and concepts to be alert for, lest they sabotage our efforts to pray before we even begin. One of the most damaging is any form of self-pity. Self-pity is destructive to our efforts to pray because it binds us to our problems, our agony about them, and our wish that we would be relieved from them. It actually becomes a form of devotion, but not devotion to God. We become addicted to feeling sorry for ourself, and this makes it all but impossible to rise out of our problems and make contact with God. Bogged down in self-pity, we are responsive only to our frustration and emotional heartburn.

A second source of subtle sabotage is the concept that God is remote and disinterested in our life and affairs. In extreme cases, we may have actually been taught to fear God and grovel with contrition in His presence. But it is even dangerous to embrace the milder idea that God is so busy taking care of the whole universe that He could not possibly have time for us. Such thinking distorts the fundamental reality of divine life—that God is alive within us as well as throughout the whole of Creation.

It is important to think of God as a benevolent power which is aware of us and concerned with helping us live our life with a greater abundance of wisdom, courage, dignity, peace, and goodwill. God is ready to provide us with support, guidance, and strength, as well as nurture the best and noblest elements within our consciousness. There are always ways we can subvert this help, but this is our own doing, not God's. Somehow, in the infinite wisdom and power which is God, God is able to support us as well as everyone else in this way. It may be difficult for some people to comprehend a concept of this magnitude, just as it is difficult for us to fully grasp any abstract aspect of life. But if we are willing to work with this basic premise, we will find that it does facilitate a deeper experience of the life of spirit through our prayers—and this is what is most important. The verification of the benevolent nature of God will come as our own spiritual experiences in prayer and living deepen.

Once our consciousness is prepared for prayer, the next step in effective prayer is *making contact with God*. If prayer was no more complicated than making a long distance call, all we would have to do would be dial the right number and wait for God to answer. But it is not this easy.

Of course, there are many people who blithely believe that "God is only a thought away." For people who have diligently learned to practice the presence of God, this is true. But these are generally not the same people! Most of the people who believe in God being just a thought away have learned only to practice the presence of *their concept of God.*

This is a problem for many of us, in fact. As a result, the challenge of contacting God is often one of penetrating past our intellectual concept of what God is—no matter how lofty or correct it may be. Once again, devotion is the all important factor. We must declare that our divine Creator truly is the supreme authority and source of life for us and devote our mind and heart and intention fully to responding to it. As we recognize this presence—no matter how poorly we may understand it—and sincerely pledge our allegiance to it, we can soar beyond our concepts and feelings about God. We will still have them, but we will be able to experience the divine forces of life to some degree as they actually are.

Of course, it is not necessary to try to contact the *whole* of God's life in order to say a simple prayer. In fact, many kinds of prayer will be far more effective if we focus primarily on the specific part of the divine life which is best suited to assist us. Not everyone will agree with this advice, however. Some people assume that God is indivisible and that we should simply contact the omnipresence of God directly, immediately, and totally. There is some merit to this idea, but it is actually more practical to realize that while God in the abstract is indivisible, the act of creation made the abstract concrete, the infinite finite. God has divided the indivisible. And our needs for divine assistance and support tend to be sharply focused in the finite challenges of daily living and growth. So it is not only reasonable but also appropriate to contact specific aspects of divine life for specific problems.

The most common aspect of God we will contact, of course, will be our own spiritual nature—our inner portion of God's life. This is the part of spirit most directly involved in our life, after all, and is certainly the part we are most attuned to. It is also our doorway to contacting the allness of God, whenever that may be necessary. Focusing on the divinity within us is not especially difficult; we simply dwell on the idea that we have been made in the image of God and that God's life, love, and wisdom are alive within the noblest and most perfect elements of our consciousness. As we extend our devotion to this force of God within us, we become responsive to it.

There will always be those who doubt how any element of divine life could possibly be present in their miserable, sinful lives, especially when they have collected so much evidence pointing to its absence. Others will be offended by any suggestion that they might have a divine presence hidden somewhere within themselves. But these objections are not serious ones. The whole purpose of seeking to live a spiritual life is to *find God and bring divine qualities into the midst of our daily life and consciousness.* If we seek the life of spirit, we must make the assumption that God is already involved in our life—not because we believe it to be so, but because God has designed us in this way and infused us with divine power and potential! And so it is both sensible and beneficial to pray to the spirit of God within us, linking our outer human nature with our hidden spiritual design.

In addition to the spirit within us, there are many other ways we can selectively attune our thoughts and aspirations to the part of divine life most suited to our particular needs. One is to address our prayer to one of the three aspects of divine life: the Father (divine will), the Mother (divine intelligence and order), or the Son (divine love). In this way, we sharpen the focus of our devotion, making it more powerful. At times, we may even want to be more specific, praying one-pointedly to divine justice, divine forgiveness, or divine strength. It depends on the purpose of our prayer.

It is also possible to pray to divine intercessors—a favorite saint, the founder of a religion, or an archangel. This is especially helpful if this saint or archangel has special knowledge or skill in working with the particular divine forces we need to contact. So we pray to this holy being to intercede on our behalf to help us link up with the appropriate power or guidance. As might be expected, the more familiar we are with this holy being—and the more we are in rapport with his or her qualities of consciousness—the more successful this kind of prayer will be.

In this regard, it should be mentioned that the major saints of any religion, Christian or otherwise, can be contacted in prayer by any sincere devotee, regardless of his or her religious beliefs or affiliation. This may be a shocking idea to certain Catholics who assume they "own" the saints—but they need to be shocked. Just as Jesus, who was a Jew, treated non-Jews and Jews with equal love and compassion, so also the real saints have transcended the religious narrowness that divide so many of the rest of us.

It is possible to take the idea of intercession to ridiculous extremes, however. Some people go so far as to pray to their friends in spirit or "spirit guides." *This practice should definitely be avoided.* Spirit guides, no matter how loving and wise, are no more divine than we are. They are human beings who have left the physical dimension of life and exist now in more subtle realms. They may be agents of God's light and love, just as we may be, but we should not ascribe to them any loftier status than this. It is perfectly proper to ask for their help at times, just as we would ask a physical friend, but we should reserve our prayers only for contact with truly divine sources.

In the same way, it is generally not a good idea to pray to one's guru or teacher. The purpose of teaching is to show us how to make our own contact with the life of spirit. It is not proper for a teacher to assume the role of divinity—or for a student to project an aura of divinity onto the teacher. Often, an intense psychic rapport will develop between student and teacher, enabling the student to ask questions and have them answered intuitively. Sometimes, the teacher may even be the avenue for answering specific prayers. But we must not confuse psychic communication with prayer. Prayer is contact with divine forces, the life of spirit. To pray effectively, we must therefore direct our prayers to bona-fide divine resources.

Once contact is made with a proper divine force, we can begin *interacting* with it. This is, obviously, the most important part of the process of prayer—our opportunity to use the time of prayer to enrich our consciousness and transform the personality. As such, the communication which occurs in prayer is meant to be far more profound than the level of communication which occurs in an ordinary phone conversation. It is not just enough to talk to God; we must listen, absorb, and respond as well. We must let the divine force we are contacting lift us out of our problem and into a new capacity to act spiritually and intelligently.

Some people might wonder, "How can all this happen in the course of reciting a four or five line prayer?" But this is not really a great mystery. The real substance of any prayer is our consciousness, not the words we speak. As we recite the words, therefore, we should focus our attention on the quality of the ideas, moods, attitudes, convictions, intentions, and values we hold on this subject. If necessary, we should pause after each sentence to build up the proper quality of consciousness to go with the words. Our goal is to use this opportunity of prayer to infuse these ideas, moods, attitudes, convictions, intentions, and values with new divine energies. This cannot happen unless we make a sincere effort to interact with these energies in our mind and heart, and through this interaction, transform our behavior and ability to act in daily life.

As important as this interaction is, nevertheless it is amazing how many people miss the point. To them, prayer is nothing but an opportunity to present a shopping list of wants and desires to God, so heaven can act on them. But this reduces the act of prayer to wish fulfillment, and robs it of its spiritual effectiveness. *Even people who would be offended by the thought that their prayers amount to nothing more than wishes all too often treat the life of spirit as something which they have defined and will use only as personal need arises.* This may be the reason why so many prayers are ineffective.

As annoying as it may be, it is nonetheless a fact that we can pray effectively only for those things that God is prepared to grant us. The power of spirit acts only in accord with divine design. When the prayer of the personality is not in harmony with this blueprint, it will not be answered. For this reason, therefore, we should always make sure that we interact first and foremost with divine will during our prayers, and only secondarily—if at all—with our wishes and desires. The great model for this aspect of prayer is Jesus praying in the Garden of Gethsemane, asking that He be spared His impending arrest and crucifixion, but adding at the end of His prayer: "Nevertheless, Thy will be done." All effective prayer includes this automatic request that divine will should override any personal requests not in harmony with it.

This injunction should not stop us, however, from praying for what we think we truly need—or what we think others need. As long as we recognize that divine intelligence holds the deciding vote as to what will happen, it is correct to proceed. And it is important to proceed, because it is often our prayer which makes it possible for divine intelligence to influence the situation. The person who is so intimidated by God's awesome power or fearful of divine retribution that he fails to pray for assistance and guidance when it is needed misses the opportunity to interact with divine life. He may also fail in his spiritual duty.

Perhaps the best rule of thumb for our interactions with divine life is that we should seldom pray for *things*, but should instead pray for our real needs—the nourishment and enrichment of our mind, emotions, body, creative ideas, work, and family. Instead of treating God as a magician who will immediately dump money and new cars on us if only we say the magic word, therefore, we begin to approach divine life as a source of abundance which can give us the opportunity to earn the money to buy the things we need. Instead of expecting God to ignore all past conditions and miraculously restore a beloved friend to perfect health, we pray that our friend become aware of the spiritual design for mental, emotional, and physical health and begin living his or her life more in accord with it, so good health can be reestablished. Instead of turning to God to deliver us from crisis—personal, national, or international—we ask the life of spirit to imbue us with the strength and wisdom to solve these difficult problems, and thereby grow. In this way, we enrich our consciousness and discover the "pearl of great price" mentioned in the New Testament. This is not a literal pearl, but rather a symbol of our true wealth—the inner wealth of divine life.

There is another good way of interacting with divine life in prayer, too, and this is to pray for divine protection against being betrayed by our own weaknesses. Our vulnerability to fear, doubt, worry, anger, sadness, inhibition, laziness, arrogance, flattery, and possessiveness causes us far more hardship than any deceit by others, external circumstance, or quirk of fate. And so it is not only proper but also a good idea to pray for the power to strengthen our self-discipline and protect ourself from what the Bible refers to as the "little foxes and rodents" which undermine our well-being and dignity.

This does not require a prolonged confession of weakness, just a quiet recognition of need. Dwelling excessively on our vulnerability to temptation or our lack of competence is always counterproductive, whether we are praying or not. It tends to energize convictions of worthlessness and inferiority, and this is not helpful. Once the request for protection from self-sabotage is made, therefore, it is important to refocus on the greater life of spirit and trust in its capacity to give us this protection.

The same kind of care must be taken when we pray on behalf of others. Even though we will usually be motivated by some genuine need of the other person, we must not dwell excessively on this need, lest we energize the difficulty. Instead, we must seek to interact with the divine love, wisdom, and power which can help resolve the difficulty. Above all, we must be sure to rise above our own *personal* thoughts and feelings about what the outcome of our prayer should be. If we fail to spend enough time developing a link with divine sources *before* making our appeal, we may do little more than project our own strong conviction about what is best for this other person. If this is the case, God may be left entirely out of the picture, thus defeating the purpose of our prayer. The one we seek to help will receive only our idea of what he or she needs!

In praying for others, therefore, it is important to work with as much detachment as possible, always asking divine love and intelligence to take charge of this effort to help. It is also beneficial to develop the excellent habit of beginning all such prayer work by rededicating ourself to the life of spirit, honoring its wisdom and love. This must be more than a token commitment which is quickly forgotten, however. It must be strong enough that it becomes a dominant and enduring part of our spiritual values.

The activity of interacting with divine life lifts our devotion and aspiration to its highest peak. When our prayer is over, however, we must take care not just to leave this focused devotion suspended, part way between heaven and earth. We must refocus our devotion, first toward elevating our normal level of thought and feeling and then toward grounding the prayer we have just completed. This is somewhat analogous to hanging up the phone in a telephone conversation and returning to other activities.

The need to "hang up" may surprise some people, but it is an important stage in praying effectively. The normal waking consciousness of most people is not filled with the measures of optimism, faith, courage, insight, and goodwill they are able to touch in prayer. In fact, it is more often a mixture of doubt, pessimism, and distress. If we are not careful, these influences may easily creep into our attitudes, adulterating the effectiveness of the prayer we have just completed.

To protect ourself from this possibility, it is a good idea to end each prayer by building a strong conviction that we have truly done something constructive through this prayer; we have tapped powerful divine forces which are already working to help us in this situation. Often, exactly this kind of thought is included at the end of prayers: "And for all the blessings given and received this moment, we give our thanks." But a tag line alone will have little effect, *unless* we charge it with the strong belief and steadfast conviction that our prayer is producing results. What we have prayed for may not be tangible or visible yet, but we have placed the order and therefore have reason to trust that delivery will be made.

There are many things in life we regularly take on trust, even though we have no proof they will happen. We call in orders to mail order houses and then wait patiently and confidently for the goods we have ordered to be delivered, even though it may take three or four weeks. And our trust is almost always justified. God is certainly not a mail order house, but the same commonsense principle does apply to prayer. It usually takes time for the forces and qualities of the life of spirit to move from the abstract dimensions where we contact them into some tangible shape in our daily life, attitudes, and behavior. We must therefore wait patiently for these influences to appear in our life, just as we would wait for an order to be delivered. *If we do not, our impatience, doubt, and pessimism may well cancel out the benefit of our prayer.*

In addition, we need to spend some time in the aftermath of our prayer deciding what we will have to do in order to ground in our daily life the spiritual forces we have tapped. We must remember that prayer is not an exercise in magic or miracles, where we turn our problem over to God and let God do the dirty work for us. Prayer is a tool for contacting the life of spirit and directing spiritual forces and resources into our life. As such, we should expect to play an active role in answering our prayers. The interaction which we establish between our personality and the life of spirit at the peak of prayer must be translated in some way into our daily life. If it is, our prayer will prove successful. If it is not, it will just be another half-finished exercise in spiritual living.

The need for participating in this way is obvious if our prayer has been for a personal benefit such as protection from our own pessimism or anxiety, but it is not so obvious in other situations—for example, if we have prayed for the resolution of a conflict with neighbors or the healing of a close friend. Nonetheless, we should expect it to be a part of making every prayer effective, because we can only receive that which we are willing to work for ourself. God always works *with* us—never for us.

This is not to say that we shoulder sole responsibility for making our prayer work. But we do shoulder some, and it varies with each prayer. It is a great responsibility if we are praying for new opportunities in our work—but much less if we are praying for the recovery of an ill person thousands of miles away. In the latter case, our responsibility for grounding our prayer may primarily be to maintain a strong faith in what we have done—and God is doing.

Once again, common sense is the best rule to follow. An effective prayer is an expression of intense devotion to some aspect of the divine life. It does not make sense to take the time to build up this kind of devotion during our moments of prayer, only to turn our back on it once the prayer is done. There is no such thing as part-time devotion. If our prayers mean anything at all, we will do what we can to help fulfill them in the physical plane.

Praying Without Ceasing

Effective prayer can never be defined as clearly and as precisely as an engineering project; the rules which govern this interaction with spirit are neither as concrete as the rules of physics nor as obvious in their application as the rules of mathematics. Nonetheless, it is important to understand that there *are* rules for praying effectively—rules that have been determined by spirit. As we study and seek to understand these rules, we come to learn that prayer is an intelligent process which should be a part of every intelligent life. Careless and sloppy efforts to pray may still produce results, because God is a god of love and mercy—but they will not be nearly as effective as intelligent prayer.

The function of prayer as a tool of spirit is that it gives us a means to deepen our relationship with God. But this must be an honest relationship, based on trust—not just our trust in God, but even more importantly our trustworthiness as an agent of God. This trustworthiness is built as we demonstrate a sense of spiritual responsibility in the way we conduct our life. *We should therefore pray only for those things that we have earned the right to ask for through our own daily experiences.*

As we *practice* goodwill and tolerance in our life, we earn the right to pray for an increase in tolerance and forgiveness—in ourself and in others as well.

As we *act* with patience and thoughtfulness, we earn the right to pray for peace—in our own life and for mankind as a whole.

As we *strive* to understand our life and do what is right, we earn the right to ask for guidance.

Prayer is not an isolated exercise which lasts a few minutes and then is finished. Its very nature establishes a relationship between the personality and God. God is interested in having this relationship endure, even if our personality is not. But the personality should be, because as we seek to harmonize our thoughts, feelings, convictions, goals, and behavior with the life of spirit, we develop a level of intimacy and trust with spirit that no mere profession of faith can equal. We make devotion an irreplaceable part of our life.

Nevertheless, many people carelessly ignore this aspect of prayer—even people who should know better. There are many people, for example, who profess to pray for peace, even though they demonstrate no understanding of peace in their own lives. There are many who pray to God to forgive others, even though they do not forgive. And there are people who pray for the fulfillment of the divine plan, even while stirring up conflict, fear, and guilt. But when these people pray, there is little they can accomplish, because they have not earned the right to ask for what they claim to be devoted to. As the Bible says, God will not be mocked.

It may seem unfair to qualify the effectiveness of prayer in this way—and the arrogant will argue we *cannot* limit God. But it is God Who sets the limits. Prayer is not an exercise in getting what we want. It is an exercise in building a stronger, more intimate relationship with divine life. And this means always striving to do the will of God. When we are able to demonstrate a measure of trustworthiness in this regard, then we have earned the right to pray for divine assistance.

As we understand this characteristic of prayer, a deeper and more profound appreciation of its value in the spiritual life gradually dawns. We begin to see that prayer is not something to be reserved only for times of crisis or special ceremony. It is an important tool in building an intimate relationship with the God within us. As such, there is virtually no end to the uses of effective prayer.

We can pray to quicken our capacity to tap and express divine qualities of devotion, tolerance, optimism, kindness, and joy. Prayers of blessing and gratitude are especially effective for this.

We can pray to be a stronger channel for intuition and inspiration, and better able to respond to divine guidance.

We can pray for a more loving heart, and thus come to know and express the divine qualities of mercy, peace, and compassion.

We can pray for better understanding of our spiritual heritage and nature, thereby strengthening our bond with God's wisdom.

We can pray to deepen our commitment to spirit, so it is continually available to us for protection from fear, doubt, and despair.

And most of all, we can pray to draw nearer to the presence of God within us.

Indeed, prayer is such an important aspect of the life of spirit that our ultimate goal should be to learn *to pray without ceasing.* And this is possible for many spiritual aspirants today. It does not mean that we would spend all our time mumbling under our breath; it simply means that the focused devotion which is the heart of all prayer should become a steady habit. It should so dominate our mind and heart and will that we would be responsive to the presence of God constantly. We would, in essence, pray ceaselessly.

This kind of devotion begins with the ordinary love and devotion of our human emotions. But as we enrich our consciousness through the repeated use of effective prayer, our devotion outgrows the personal focus of our emotions and becomes a force which magnetically attracts to us the presence of spiritual love that is the heart of all phenomena of life. This then combines with our own love to form a divine amalgam of unwavering devotion.

But even this devotion needs to be focused. As we come into contact with the full spectrum of life, we need to look through the eyes of love and register the innate divinity which is the heart of everyone and everything, even our adversaries. And we need to recognize that this is the same life of spirit that we appeal to every time we pray. It is the perfect pattern for love, growth, and health in this person or object, and by working with it to help it emerge, we fulfill the responsibility we incur when we pray.

We pray not just to a transcendent God, a God Who will work behind the scenes to give us what we cannot give ourself. We pray to the God Who is the heart of every living thing—the heart of all life. Thus, every thought we think, every emotion we express, and every act we make can be a prayer.

This is the goal of praying without ceasing.

Invoking Divine Life

Awake And Ready To Act

*L*ife is built on principles which often seem paradoxical. One of the greatest of these "paradoxes" is the fact that while change is an ever-present ingredient of life, most of us are so thoroughly controlled by habit and tradition that genuine change hardly occurs at all. The superficial elements of life change, but our basic character traits and values remain virtually the same. We meet new people, pursue new career directions, and perhaps even embark on a new lifestyle—yet do not change the way in which we treat others, approach our work, or fulfill our responsibilities.

Even when challenged by crisis, our human nature seems to resist change, retreating instead into defensiveness and greater selfishness. Instead of seizing the opportunity of crisis to look at life from a more enlightened perspective and cultivate nobler attitudes and ethics, we learn only to manipulate our environment and other people more skillfully—to avoid problems and to shift responsibility for our failures to others. This adroit reshuffling of people and situations may seem to make us stronger and bring us a temporary advantage—but it blinds us to the fact that we are not changing in any significant way, just the world around us. Sooner or later, therefore, we will find that we have been left behind.

Some people, of course, seem to take comfort in remaining the same while the rest of life changes, but these people suffer from a cruel form of self-delusion. While habit and tradition do give consistency and pattern to our life, we are meant to control our habits and modify them as appropriate, not be a slave to them. When any habit becomes so strong that it traps us in a cycle of endless repetition, we have outgrown its usefulness. It is time for a change—but not a change in circumstance alone. Far more importantly, it is time for a change in our character and behavior. Instead of trying to solve our problems by forcing others and life itself to change, it is time to learn that *we are the one who must change.*

Yet genuine change can seem hard to achieve, especially if we have become addicted to custom and habit. The momentum of our habits can be a powerful tyrant which successfully resists sincere transformation of character and behavior. Nevertheless, the principles of life cannot be mocked. No matter how strong the resistance of our habits and traditions may be, the spiritual force of growth is even stronger. The more we ignore making changes in the way we treat others, the more we run up against difficult relationships which wear off the rough edges of our reactiveness. The more we refuse to invest our talents and intelligence forthrightly in our work, the more we are passed over "unfairly" for promotions, until we realize that we ought to be doing more to earn the advancement we seek. The more we approach life with fear and anxiety, the more we encounter periods of prolonged distress which teach us the need for calmness, poise, and courage. And the more we rationalize our behavior and apologize for our lapses of integrity, the more we are forced to face the emptiness within us.

Unfortunately, when we allow the conflict between resistance and growth to rage unabated in these ways, we suffer enormously. And unnecessarily, too, because each of us possesses within us a rich inner heritage which we could call on at any time to help us face these crises—our spiritual power to grow. Yet as rich and abundant as the inner life is, and as ready as it always is to help us face and resolve our problems, it is amazing how few of us—even those of us who are on the spiritual path—tap and utilize this abundance. Given the choice between acting with a new measure of nobility and dignity or repeating the mistakes we have made so many times in the past, all too often we ignore the new and cling to the old. Given the choice between the human experience of anger and defensiveness and the spiritual experience of goodwill and cooperation, we shun the spiritual and reinforce the human. We miss the chance to grow.

The paradoxes and conflicts of human life cannot be resolved in strictly human terms. Instead, we must lift our eyes above the personal level of daily life and tap the abundance of the life of spirit. In this way, we are able to shake ourself loose from the ruts of old habits and traditions and move forward into new opportunities. Indeed, we regularly face situations and problems which are *designed* to compel us to rise up to the level of spirit and harness the highest elements of life within us—situations and problems which can only be solved by using the tools of spirit.

The tools of spirit are never more helpful to us than in enabling us to outgrow the old and worn-out and replace them with the new and spiritual. The tool of prayer helps us focus our heartfelt devotion to the ideal and seek out the strength and presence of God to assist us. Confession permits us to make a proper alignment with spirit and recognize it as a source of new life which can guide and direct us. Meditation gives us a means of attuning ourself to the life of spirit and integrating its qualities into our character.

Of all the tools of spirit, however, the one which is the most vital to this process of breaking through our resistance to growth is *invocation*. Through the proper use of invocation, we can summon our spiritual treasures of wisdom, courage, goodwill, patience, and joy to help us face our daily problems and needs. Instead of blundering by trial and error through problems we do not understand, we can invoke wisdom to help us comprehend them and act effectively. Instead of exhausting our personal will by trying to persevere in difficult circumstances, we can invoke spiritual strength not only to help us endure but actually become a force of healing and strength to others. Instead of letting the resentment of some injury or insult fester year after year, as we strain to muster the courage to forgive, we can invoke divine love and goodwill to help us cleanse away this hurt and refocus our efforts constructively.

Indeed, as we master this tool of spirit, we will find that invocation has many marvelous uses in bringing selected elements of heaven to earth and focusing them effectively in our life. Yet as versatile and as important as this tool of spirit is, it is perhaps the least known and used of all the tools. Even many spiritual aspirants fail to use the remarkable power of invocation to assist them in their work of contacting and applying the forces of spirit. In part, this is due to the legacy of passiveness which has stifled the spiritual scene for the last several thousand years. All too many aspirants are content simply to adore God and rest in the vague expectation that divine providence will bless them in some useful way. They do not inject themselves into the process of actually summoning divine force or learning the skills required to focus it, harness it, and express it. Yet this is naïveté at its worst, for most of the major breakthroughs of spiritual progress come as the result of invoking new life of spirit as we struggle with our problems. If we are not skilled and practiced in using the tool of invocation, we will miss many opportunities to grow as a spiritual person.

There are two ways we can summon assistance from divine sources. We can make a general appeal, knowing that we need help but leaving it to higher intelligence to figure out what we need and how to deliver it. Or, we can make a specific appeal, knowing precisely what we need, the capacity of the inner life to provide it, and what we must do to channel and express it once we receive it. Each way can produce spectacular results. But it should be obvious that the second way greatly expands our capacity to interact with divine forces and bring them into expression on earth. This is the power of invocation.

Invocation can be used either to enrich our own efforts or to help other people, groups, and even the world as a whole. Individually, there are many times every day when we could increase our effectiveness and accelerate our growth if only we would invoke an extra measure of wisdom, strength, or love to guide and support us. If we practice invocation in this way, then we will also be able to use it effectively on those occasions when we are confronted by a crisis of serious proportion.

Using invocation to summon divine force for the benefit of others and the nations of the world is an even greater use of this tool. We are not just an isolated individual with no opportunity to help the world grow and develop sanely; as we grow in spiritual stature, we come to realize that we are a cell in the body of humanity. As such, we are able to invoke help for any other member of the same body—or for the body as a whole. And if we can focus specifically on the divine force or spiritual quality needed—through the intelligent use of invocation—then the impact we can have can be tremendous. We can summon the forces of wisdom, strength, love, justice, peace, joy, order, and patience to infuse a difficult situation and lift up the minds and hearts of those involved, so that they respond more fully to the goodness and nobility within them.

Why is invocation such a powerful tool for summoning the presence of spiritual qualities and forces? Because whenever we truly invoke the life of spirit, *we are calling forth that which is there and ready to respond.* We are not just asking for divine intervention or blind help, without knowing if it is there or able to act. On the contrary: having explored and discovered the many elements of the life of God, we are focusing on a specific quality, flooding our awareness with it, then summoning it to infuse our own life or the lives of those we seek to help. Knowing it is there, we call it forth to appear on earth.

To appreciate this subtle point fully, we must understand that *invocation* is the inseparable partner of *evocation.* Invocation is the act of *calling forth* from heaven some aspect of the life of spirit so we can express it on earth. It is the act of the personality summoning a response from spirit. Evocation, by contrast, is the act of our spiritual nature *calling forth* a specific response from the personality. Through evocation, God summons us to cooperate more fully in the work of manifesting our spiritual design for living—to learn more about the life of spirit and what we can do to harness and express the power and qualities of spirit more fully in our daily life.

Invocation is a powerful tool of spirit for a very simple reason: by the time we have identified a need, realized that we require divine assistance, and formulated an invocation for help from spirit, we are well on our way to responding to the evocation of our spiritual self. In other words, an effective invocation will always be our response to a corresponding evocation. An intelligent invocation is never a desperate cry in the wilderness. It is always an answer—an answer to the evocation of spirit. We may think we must awaken spirit to a recognition of our great need, but it is in fact spirit which has been trying for some time to awaken us. Our invocation indicates that we are, at last, awake—and ready to act.

This is the reason why invocation is so effective in helping us break down our barriers to growth—our resistance, inertia, and defensiveness. As our habits and mistakes have been repeated, cycle after cycle, spirit has been trying to call forth from us a more intelligent understanding of our problems. But the average human personality can be quite adept at ignoring the summons—until the summoner finds a way to deliver it so it cannot be ignored. If we learn to invoke help and guidance at the first sign of difficulty, instead of waiting for the final sign of catastrophe, we can more quickly respond to the summons.

Through the twin processes of evocation and invocation, the personality and spirit begin acting together, in harmony. To some extent, these twin processes operate automatically as we tread the spiritual path. But as with all the tools of spirit, we should never take the work of invocation and evocation for granted, just because they sometimes do work automatically. If we learn to use this tool intelligently and consciously, we can greatly increase its power in our life. We can use it to invoke specific qualities we need for our daily activities; to invoke the ideal plan or resolution for trying circumstances; to harness the forces we need for healing and blessing; to call forth creative ideas and inspired insights; and to summon the proper and orderly unfoldment of complex projects or enterprises.

In fact, invocation can be so powerful that it may seem as though it were a form of magic. None of the tools of spirit, however, should be regarded as a way of working magic. Magic implies the suspension of divine or physical laws. Invocation works within the context of divine law. It never responds to human whim or vanity, except to expose it.

This likewise means that we must be ready and willing to serve as an agent of the forces we summon. Invocation is not meant to be a means for asking God to do our dirty work for us! If we invoke wisdom, we must learn to interpret and apply it intelligently. If we summon divine love, we must learn to use it to transform our attitudes and behavior into expressions of goodwill and helpfulness. If we invoke divine peace to help calm quarrelling factions within a group, we must still do what we can to serve as a peacemaker.

If we are willing to cooperate with the forces we invoke, then we will tap the real promise of invocation—its capacity to link heaven and earth, *through us*. In a very real sense, we will become the "missing piece" which resolves the paradox and demonstrates that the seeming conflict between heaven and earth is more illusion than reality. Heaven constantly calls on us, through evocation, and expects us to call on it, through invocation. In this way, a genuine communication is established and we are able to participate more fully in the grand drama of our growth and spiritual unfoldment.

The Law Of Reciprocity

To master the tool of invocation, we must learn to use it wisely. It is not enough just to focus our devotion on the presence of God and hope that divine forces will assist us; by its very nature, invocation requires the one who calls on heaven to choose the specific spiritual forces he intends to work with and to manage them skillfully. We should therefore clearly understand the importance of intelligence to the work of invocation. In fact, the very first step in learning to invoke properly should be to learn how the universe works and the role we play in it.

We need to *understand,* not just believe, that the universe has a spiritual design and purpose which governs its unfoldment—and that this is a design which embraces our life, too.

We need to *understand,* not just believe, that we live in an orderly universe which is designed to respond to this divine plan and fulfill it.

And we need to *understand,* not just believe, that we are designed to become an intelligent channel for spiritual purpose—a steward of the plan to spiritualize human nature and civilization. Because we are designed to act in this way, we have a right to invoke this divine plan whenever we seek to serve as an agent of it.

Unfortunately, most of us neither understand this design of life nor act in accord with it. Instead, most of us are accustomed to reacting haphazardly to the circumstances of life, as though personal wishes and whims were the only important factors to consider. Our orientation is self-centered. Our vision is materialistic. Our sense of purpose is selfish rather than noble. Our habits are focused in gaining pleasure and avoiding all distress. And our goals are framed primarily in self-indulgence, the acquisition of power and fame, and our personal ability to control the world about us.

The average person, in supreme arrogance, views the universe as something to ignore, because he does not regard it as alive or involved in his life. The modern doctrines of nihilism and existentialism which have trivialized philosophy reinforce this arrogant assumption. Even when the universe is recognized as a force to be dealt with, it is usually regarded by the average person as a random, unstructured force to be manipulated to his advantage—or as a friendly but dull-witted Santa Claus who is ready to give and give and give at the slightest request.

Of course, none of these views of the universe is accurate. There are divine designs and patterns for living, and the intelligent person always seeks to understand them and cooperate with them. The fabric of life in which we live and move and have our being is intelligent, structured, and organized. As we discover our own personal heritage of intelligence, discipline, and order, we learn to invoke these patterns to assist us in our work, relationships, and growth. But this means we must be able to discern the difference between patterns of intelligence and mere fantasies or wishes. If we try to invoke peace or wisdom or love from an utopian fantasy, we will get no response. It has no power—no capacity to evoke growth from us. If we try to invoke a mature solution to one of our problems from our personal desires and wishes, once again we will get no worthwhile response. Our wishes and desires have no spiritual power—no ability to evoke maturity from us.

To cultivate the discernment we need in order to invoke the life of spirit successfully, we must recognize that the invocation of fantasies and wishes is something to be left to children, who love to play games of make believe. As a spiritual adult, we must leave the games of children behind and learn to work impersonally—responding first to the patterns and designs of universal life, and only secondarily to our perceived personal needs and wishes. For as long as we are motivated by personal wishes and longings, we will not be operating on a wavelength on which we can hear the evocation of the soul—and respond with an intelligent invocation.

Let us therefore examine the spiritual and psychological designs which make invocation and evocation possible. Both individually and collectively, there is a continuous interplay between heaven and earth. For a long, long time, we are unaware of this interplay, blinded by our involvement in the mundane aspects of life. But it is there, at work in our life, because spirit has always been involved, directly and indirectly, in the affairs of the physical plane, seeking to impel the personality on to new growth and greater awareness. From the outset, spirit has worked from a comprehensive plan, in harmony with universal law. As we have responded to its efforts and grown in consciousness, we have done our part in perpetuating this constant interplay.

The continuous interaction of heaven and earth in our life is a demonstration of the law of reciprocity at work. This principle, which is also known as the law of correspondences, states that all phenomena of life have an inner or transcendent cause—and that every spiritual force has some influence on outer events and appearances. Changes occurring at inner levels eventually produce corresponding changes at the outer level. And changes occurring at the outer level will either enrich or restrict the ability of spirit to control and direct its expression on earth.

More simply put, the patterns and purposes of spirit shape and condition the opportunities, temperament, and activities of the personality. And our values, convictions, attitudes, and behavior reflect, even if imperfectly, some measure of our spiritual life. Even though spirit may not dominate or control the personality, it is nevertheless a primary conditioning influence on our character and behavior.

At the same time, the personality has a reciprocal influence on the efforts of spirit to shape it. Our state of mind, the quality of our emotions, and the nature of our behavior will directly affect the nature of our relationship with spirit. If we think and act in noble, intelligent, and loving ways, we strengthen our character and summon corresponding qualities from spirit. But if we think and act selfishly, materialistically, and defensively, we weaken our character. Yet even this type of activity draws a response from spirit, as it seeks to correct our indiscretions and lapses in integrity. We are still summoning the life of spirit—we just do not realize it.

In most people, the continuous interplay of spirit and personality is an invisible process which can only be observed indirectly, by examining the subtle hand of spirit guiding the events of life and the development of character. In all too many people, in fact, the handiwork of spirit is hard to find in ordinary ways, such as the way they treat others, pursue their work, or define their priorities. The involvement of spirit in the life of the personality can only be ascertained by examining its influence on the long-term evolution of character. The plan is there, but it is hard to trace its execution.

It is only in a small number of people that the interplay of spirit and personality is readily discernible. Yet these are the people who teach us that invocation is possible. There *are* heavenly forces available to us which we can call forth from heaven and focus on earth, to help us meet the challenges of living and solve our problems. And when they are summoned and held in intelligent focus, these forces are strong enough and powerful enough to shape earthly conditions and phenomena.

The study of the interplay between heaven and earth, both individually and collectively, is the *science* of invocation and evocation. To comprehend invocation properly, we must approach it in this context. It is not just a tool for bringing heaven to earth; far more importantly, it is a dynamic part of the relationship between spirit and personality. Personality cannot exist without spirit. Invocation cannot occur without evocation. And the mature use of invocation is always reciprocal in nature.

It is most informative to understand how thoroughly reciprocity shapes human life and psychology. Just being curious about what is happening around us can invoke ideas, insights, and inspiration about the events of our life and the people we know. Treating other people with affection and goodwill likewise can become a summons of the best within them.

Not all examples of reciprocity in human psychology are as positive as these, however. People who are chronically pessimistic and fearful tend to summon precisely the type of condition they condemn or fear. Moreover, their attitude conjures up a gloomy mood which follows them wherever they go, so that even if they happen to attract more favorable circumstances, they are unable to enjoy them. Their gloominess and fear also tend to call forth the pessimism and irritation latent in other people. In this way, their pessimistic cycle repeats itself endlessly. Angry and rude people likewise summon the worst in themselves and others. As they give vent to their anger, they magnify their irritability and energize their reactiveness. And by their words and behavior, they provoke resentment and retaliation in others.

Such behavior is not an *invocation*, since nothing is being called from heaven to earth; it would more appropriately be called a *provocation*. It is behavior which is designed to provoke a reaction from others, either deliberately or unintentionally. And because the principle of reciprocity infuses human psychology as well as the relationship between the soul and the personality, this type of provocation does indeed draw a response. Action leads to reaction; stimulus is followed by response.

Human beings are complex. We have the potential to be angry as well as tolerant, patient as well as irritated, clearheaded as well as confused, trusting as well as skeptical. But unless we are guided by an awareness of the plans and designs of spirit, we are likely to be perfectly predictable in our complexity. Under the law of reciprocity, a provocation will incite a reaction of similar quality unless specifically modified by a disciplined choice. In other words, anger will provoke resentment, unless we choose to respond with tolerance and goodwill. Impatience will provoke irritation, unless we choose to respond with patience.

This principle works to our benefit as well, of course. Cheerfulness will tend to elicit happiness in others. Affection will provoke kindness and greater affection. But it must be understood that even this is a provocation, not an invocation. The principle of reciprocity behaves in similar ways in both invocation and provocation, but the phenomena are quite different. It is a difference in focus, as illustrated by the following diagram:

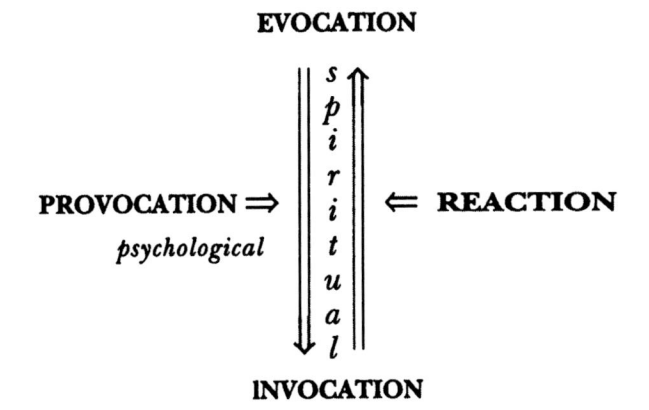

EVOCATION

PROVOCATION ⇒ *spiritual* ⇐ **REACTION**
psychological

INVOCATION

The interplay of provocation and reaction is horizontal; it occurs entirely at the level of the personality. It characterizes the interactions of ordinary people, but does not lead to any kind of genuine progress. It simply sets in motion repeated cycles of provocation and reaction. The interplay of invocation and evocation, on the other hand, is vertical; it links our needs on earth with the spiritual resources of heaven. As a result, *we cannot truly invoke anything unless we are prepared to grow.* For just as soon as our invocation has been uttered, an evocation stirs within our awareness and character. Spirit calls on us to grow so that we will be better prepared to handle the new force we have invoked.

Spirit's response to our invocation—its evocation of us—differs greatly from the average reaction to a psychological provocation. We can learn, after all, to control our psychological reactions; we do not have to respond to a hostile provocation by being hostile ourself. But we cannot control the way an evocation will work upon us in response to a genuine invocation. Once we invoke, we must be ready to act.

There are many good examples of what this means to us. If we are in a situation where we are being treated unfairly, for instance, we can invoke divine justice to help us reestablish fairness for all. But the divine justice we invoke in this way is a powerful, impersonal force. It will not just overshadow and correct the misbehavior of those who are treating us unfairly; it will expose all unfairness, even our own. So when we invoke divine justice, we must be prepared to grow in our own awareness of justice and become an agent of this spiritual force ourself.

Similarly, if we are confused and bewildered, we can invoke our spiritual resources of wisdom to help us see more clearly. But the response of spirit to our request will not be a blinding flash of illumination which reveals all we need to know. Far more likely, spirit will respond by demonstrating to us more forcefully than ever the illusions and self-deceptions within our thinking and priorities which distort our understanding, prodding us to replace them with new values, insights, and convictions.

Invocation, in other words, is nearly inseparable from evocation. If we try to approach it in terms of provocation—in terms of how we can get spirit to do what we want it to do—it will inevitably backfire. Instead, we must work from the top down, trying to understand what spirit is trying to evoke from us.

Our interests often tend to be self-centered and personal. We want help in getting a promotion at work, assistance in making our relationships more fulfilling, and support in achieving our goals and growth as painlessly as possible. The interests of spirit tend to be substantially different—impersonal, altruistic. Spirit is more interested in the growth of our talents and dedication than in specific promotions; in increased cooperation and goodwill in relationships than in personal fulfillment; and in genuine contributions to the quality of human life than in the attainment of personality goals. This does not mean that we should forget about our promotions, self-fulfillment, and goals; it simply means we need to shift our priorities so that we place what we want in the context of what spirit wants. We need to put the principle of reciprocity to work intelligently in our own life.

As the ancient truism says, "As above, so below." As we call down the forces of heaven to help us on earth, we add to our spiritual potential, either individually or collectively.

Unless our invocation is motivated by a sincere intent to grow, it does not make any sense to call on heaven for help. The Apostle Paul wrote, "All the things of the earth reveal the invisible nature of God." The invisible nature he refers to is nothing less than the spiritual design for all things. As we master the tool of invocation, we learn to call this design into manifestation.

We, too, become an agent who reveals the invisible nature of God.

Learning To Invoke

The work of invocation is possible because the universe is alive and organized in such a way that it sustains harmony among all its parts. At some primordial level, divine will is at work behind all creation, charging it with the energies which drive the mechanism of creation and impel the evolution of the divine plan for it. We, as part of creation, have access to this source of life as we assume our spiritual role as an agent of the divine plan.

Our capacity to invoke divine forces is triggered by accepting this role as a meaningful one in our life—by recognizing that we are part of a cosmic design which is the very fabric of the universe. As a citizen of a living universe, we have an obligation to accept its laws and plans. If we can grasp this fact to some degree, then it will be relatively easy to master the basics of invocation. Once again, however, it must be stressed that the work of invocation requires a well-trained, enlightened mind. Belief and faith in a living, intelligent universe are not enough to make invocation work with reliability; we must add wisdom to our belief and skill to our faith. We therefore have an obligation to study the principles of the science of invocation and evocation and develop a solid mental structure of convictions, values, and plans which will become the "launching pad" for our invocations of spirit and spirit's evocations of us.

The best way to build this mental structure is in our own life first. Just as God has an evolutionary plan for the whole universe, so also our own soul has a design and purpose for our life. For invocation to work in our life, we must understand something of this design and purpose and translate its key elements into our priorities, values, interests, and behavior. Once we have made substantial progress in building this enlightened mental structure for our own life, then we can also broaden our scope, to include the divine plan for all life as well.

In trying to understand our spiritual design and purpose, however, we must take care not to be distracted by unproductive side issues. Many spiritual aspirants waste a lot of time pursuing a deeper understanding of their "purpose in life" by looking for something glamorous rather than real. They think of their purpose as some master secret which will give them the key to living—rather than as a practical guide to spiritual responsibility. Purpose is never this complex. We can gain a great deal of insight into our spiritual purpose by reflecting on our dual nature as spirit and personality and how they interact. In this way, we can see that:

Spirit guides, and the personality follows.
Spirit impels, and the personality responds.
Spirit directs, and the personality acts.
Spirit empowers, and the personality expands the scope of its activities.
Spirit inspires, and the personality grows in wisdom.

Spirit invests its compassion, and the personality expresses goodwill.

Spirit leads, and the personality serves.

The design and purpose of spirit for our life will be framed in global ideas such as these, not in specific revelations about events in our life or struggles we have endured. The events and struggles of our life are important, but primarily in the context of whether or not we have used them to respond to spirit. Have we used these occasions to let spirit guide us, inspire us, and impel us? Have we responded by increasing our expression of goodwill, wisdom, and strength? If we have, then we have been aware of our spiritual design and purpose and have acted on it. But if we have retreated into selfishness, defensiveness, anger, and materialism instead, then we have been led by our human, not our spiritual, nature.

As we examine the purpose and design of our life in this way, we must then use the insights we gain as a basis for building new values, setting new priorities, and refocusing our behavior. We must incorporate into our thinking the fundamental reality that spiritual force does flow from heaven to earth and is vital to our well-being. In specific, we must realize that:

• Because the soul is charged with divine will, we have an inner purpose we are meant to fulfill.

• Because the soul is the residence of spiritual wisdom, we are able to make sense of this purpose and design.

• Because the soul is made of love, we can tap the power we need to infuse goodwill into our character and behavior.

As we build an appropriate mental structure for our invocations, we will begin to realize that we have often successfully invoked the soul—and been evoked by it—even though we may not have recognized it at the time. There have been times when we have needed an extra measure of courage, tolerance, guidance, or skill, *and it has come to us and helped us,* once we identified our specific need. We may be surprised how quietly the help arrived—spirit generally acts without fanfare or spectacle. But we will know, as we build our understanding and skill, that invocation is a process we can rely on. And these insights into the workings of the soul will help us revise our concepts of invocation and evocation, making them more practical and useful. A genuine invocation is not a desperate appeal for a miracle which will rescue us from deep trouble; it is an intelligent appeal for specific spiritual forces which will help us better fulfill our inner purpose.

Once this mental structure has been properly built and is in place in our daily thinking, feeling, and behavior, then the actual use of invocation in specific situations can proceed. At all times, however, we should keep in mind that the process of invocation is really the twin processes of invocation and evocation. In fact, one of the best ways to approach any situation in life is to ask ourself: "What is the soul evoking in me through this challenge or problem?"

Few of us ever ask ourself this question—but we ought to. We need to pause on a regular basis and wonder: what is the soul trying to teach me through my work, relationships, and responsibilities? What opportunities is spirit busy arranging for me—and how will I have to change, in conviction, attitude, and action, in order to seize them? How does the soul expect me to change so I can better cooperate with it?

What are the dominant forces of spirit I need to work with at this point in time?

If we begin thinking about any situation in this context, it will be relatively easy to identify our real need for help. We will be thinking in the context of spiritual purpose, not personal desire. All too many people, however, do not go beyond a personal framework of thinking in identifying their needs. Instead of defining what they need in terms of the soul, they define it in the most personal, selfish, defensive, and materialistic ways. They make up a "shopping list" of their wants and desires, then expect spirit to deliver it.

In times of stress, for example, most people define their "need" simply in terms of being rid of their stress—or at least being rid of the feeling of distress. If they are under great pressure at work, they think their need is for a better, more fulfilling job. If they are no longer satisfied with their marriage, they think their need is for someone who will care more deeply for them, treat them with great affection, or give them a more romantic thrill. But from the perspective of the soul, these are just palliatives—something the personality would *like*.

The *need* of the personality is for new measures of maturity, wisdom, goodwill, and courage.

When we analyze our problems and hardships only in terms of what the personality would like, we create a repeating cycle of frustration. We end up believing that the only way our situation in life can improve is if others make changes in the way they treat us, if society comes to our rescue, or if God should magically send us assistance in some other form. We may cry out for help, but help will not come, because we have not defined a genuine need. We are taunting the universe, daring it to help us, rather than invoking spiritual guidance, wisdom, and love.

Let it be clearly understood: we cannot hope to define our true need in any situation unless we comprehend that the resolution to our problems *will come from within us.* We must be willing to respond to the evocation of the soul and grow in our ability to solve our problems before we will be able to understand what it is we need of spirit.

Indeed, one of the fundamental principles of invocation is that we cannot call forth from spirit anything which spirit does not want to—

or cannot—send to us. Spirit is not willing to help us become a tyrant in our household or business; if we ask it to make everyone bow down to our wishes and commands, it will refuse. Nor is spirit going to shower us with all the material comforts we might be tempted to request—especially if these material comforts would have to be gained at the expense of others. Spirit will not arrange for a promotion we do not deserve, nor a windfall we have not earned. But if we are ready to grow, we can summon spirit to strengthen us with the qualities of character and the divine forces we need. If we are awake to the new directions in which spirit is leading us, we will find invocation a powerful tool.

Some situations, of course, are so complex that it is difficult to ascertain clearly just what quality of spirit is needed. In such cases, we must try to extract from the complexity the basic spiritual purposes and themes which ought to be governing our involvement, and then identify our true need in this context. The cold war arms race, for instance, not only poses complex problems for the nations involved, but also reflects even greater conflicts within the whole of humanity. To invoke a simplistic solution—that all the nations destroy their bombs and stop making any more—is naïve. It is tantamount to asking for a miracle which would smash all bombs and munition factories, but leave unresolved the underlying conflicts which cause nations to build bombs and contemplate using them.

If we rise above this simplistic level, however, we can put the arms race into its proper context—the context of human conflict and what it means. One of the meanings of persistent conflict is that it evokes us to search for and find new ways of creating and establishing harmony and cooperation. In this light, we can then understand that the spiritual purpose to be extracted from the arms race is the need to nurture right human relationships at a global level—among groups of nations, not just individuals. And more importantly, we can see that if there is no improvement at this level, then the simplistic act of taking away bombs and missiles will not lead to peace. As long as the underlying conflict exists, nations will continue to fight, one way or another—with sticks and rocks, if not with bombs and missiles! And so, to halt the arms race, we would need to invoke goodwill, patience, a sense of unity among all people, and intelligent solutions to the conflicts which rage among the nations. We must act mentally, not emotionally or physically.

Once we have intelligently defined our true need in these ways, we are then ready to take the next step in the process of invocation—attunement to spirit. It is important not to take this step for granted. Some people do naïvely assume that their merest wish is sufficient to attract the attention of spirit, while others presume that faith alone will put them in instant rapport with divine forces. But intelligent people understand that attunement with spirit is difficult to achieve and sustain, and therefore needs our constant attention.

Most importantly, our need for improvement must be *heartfelt*. As we yearn for the specific quality of spiritual force that we need, we must create a tension between our human and spiritual natures which draws in the life of spirit. This is not tension in the sense of conflict, but rather the tension of being poised, filled with expectation, and ready to act.

This tension must infuse the whole of our

personality—our thoughts, intentions, and emotions—so that our whole being is devoted to attracting the power and presence of spirit. Mentally, we build our tension by anticipating the quality of force we need and by contemplating the ways we will use it when it arrives. At the level of our will, we harness tension by dedicating ourself to working to resolve this problem and by focusing a strong determination to act intelligently and constructively. And by focusing our emotions to aspire to greater wisdom, strength, self-discipline, and compassion, we likewise contribute to the vital process of creating a proper level of tension for our invocation.

Some might argue that these steps in attunement are just psychological maneuvers. Yet they do invoke the life of spirit quite effectively—assuming we have already taken other steps to cultivate a working relationship with spirit. It is not even necessary to think of ourself as spiritual or religious in a formal sense; a dedication to helping others and being a constructive force in life is usually enough to build some kind of working relationship with spirit.

Nonetheless, as true as this is, there are some people who do think of themselves as spiritual or religious, yet have little success in invoking the life of spirit. This is because they do not use the whole of their personality as an attracting force. In most cases, their entire relationship with spirit has been based on the passive adoration of God, focused in the emotions. They have no real experience in actively working to bring spiritual qualities to earth or serving as their agent. They know how to feel good about God—but they do not know how to help God fulfill the divine plan.

Invocation does require greater involvement than just ordering a pizza to be delivered to our door. We must prepare ourself by defining the quality we need. Then, as we formulate our fixed intention, focus our expectation, build our determination, and add a strong aspiration to succeed, we sound forth a powerful summons that brings heaven to earth. Without this mental preparation and intense dedication to serve as an agent of the incoming forces, however, our invocation would be nothing more than a pile of words.

Yet even building a proper level of tension

is not enough; we must sustain this level of tension throughout the whole process of invocation. This can be accomplished by using seed thoughts in a meditative state. A seed thought is a clear mental focus on a specific spiritual quality. As we concentrate on this quality in active meditation, working with the certain conviction that the immediate source of this quality is our soul, we open the door for spirit to charge our thought-form with large quantities of spiritual power.

This stage of the process can be illustrated by the example of a person who tends to procrastinate too much. Thinking about this problem, he recognizes that his true need is for more self-discipline. He attunes himself to his soul, knowing it to be a fount of great self-determination, then focuses his attention mentally, concentrating on the spiritual power to make enlightened choices in life and building his conviction that he can conquer his tendency to procrastinate by increasing his self-discipline.

Holding the seed thought of self-discipline up to the light of the soul in this way is like holding a chalice of our heartfelt need up to heaven, so that the life of spirit can fill it. And this is basically what happens as a result of our invocation. Our character is infused with the new life and power of spiritual purpose. This new life and power pour into our mind and heart consciously—but also create a reservoir of spiritual force at unconscious levels. In this way, we charge up our spiritual batteries and are able to draw on this vitality and power whenever we need to in the future.

Once we have translated the spiritual forces we are invoking into seed thoughts and then into a reservoir of unconscious force, it is relatively easy to transfer them into mental values, plans, and convictions. For example, we can use our creative imagination to think of specific habits and values being charged by these forces. Or we can use standard meditative techniques of integration to incorporate the qualities of these forces into our self-image, attitudes, and habits.

If we tend to be cynical and distrustful, for instance, we could invoke the spiritual qualities of goodwill and generosity. Having built up seed thoughts which embody these forces, we can then direct the power of these seed thoughts at our own attitudes toward other people, seeing how our customary attitudes of cynicism and distrust have alienated us from the goodness in others and recognizing how new attitudes of affection, kindness, and helpfulness will be much more in tune with the spiritual forces we have invoked. By working repeatedly in this way, the old patterns of cynicism and distrust are jettisoned from our character and replaced by new capacities for goodwill and generosity.

This final step of invocation can be made even more powerful if we then harness the force we have contacted to *bless* the situation as it now exists, knowing we have released powerful energies which are at work to improve it. The object is to bless the spiritual potential already at work in the situation with the full force of the spiritual quality we have invoked. In other words, we would bless our potential for growth with the force of spiritual goodwill or wisdom—or the corresponding potential for growth in our friends, the groups we belong to, or humanity as a whole.

In this way, we complete our alignment with the perspective and purposes of spirit.

Putting Invocation To Work

As is true with any tool of spirit, invocation can only become a practical part of our life *if we use it*. Fortunately, the uses and applications of invocation are many—in fact, they are as varied and diverse as spirit itself. The only limits to our use of invocation would be our own capacity to recognize need, the time we spend on contacting and interacting with spirit, and our ability to receive and express the spiritual energies we invoke.

In invoking divine life, we need to remember that we are simultaneously being evoked by spirit to *come to its aid* in implementing some aspect of its spiritual design. From the beginning, therefore, we should cultivate the habit of using invocation only to respond to spiritual need—not our personal wishes. Furthermore, we must understand that we can only invoke that for which we are willing to assume responsibility. If we are habitually a troublemaker, we have no right to invoke peace—until we begin to make an honest effort to serve as a peacemaker. This is no arbitrary rule of a capricious creator; it is an integral part of the process of invocation. In order to invoke effectively, we must *put our whole personality and self-expression* in harmony with spirit. Anything at odds with the purpose of spirit will diminish the force of our invocation. In using other tools of spirit, it is possible to achieve partial success even while portions of the personality are not in harmony with spirit. But this is not true of invocation; *we can only invoke those forces that we are already trying to cultivate in our own thoughts, convictions, and behavior.* The reason why is simple: the act of invocation calls forth the qualities and forces of spirit, not finite results on the physical plane. In order to translate these qualities and forces into the finite results we desire, we must act as an agent for the life of spirit. This cannot happen unless our mind and behavior form an effective channel for spiritual self-expression.

Understanding this, the logical place to start practicing the use of invocation is to accelerate our growth. We can, for instance, invoke any of the treasures of spirit to strengthen weak areas of our character. If we chronically lack assertiveness, we can invoke a fresh measure of the courage to act on our convictions. If we are often discouraged and apathetic, we can invoke joy and a stronger sense of purpose to give meaning and add enthusiasm to our life. If we are frequently sluggish and lacking in vitality, we can invoke the strength of spirit to charge up the vigor of our convictions, attitudes, and physical health.

Individual uses of invocation will naturally vary from person to person, depending upon individual need. It is perfectly proper to invoke help in meeting the challenges of daily living—new insights for work, greater patience in dealing with relatives, or fresh resolve for changing bad habits—so long as we always focus our use of invocation in terms of approaching these mundane problems with new spiritual resources. As we gain expertise in solving this kind of problem, however, it is likely that our use of invocation will shift, so that it becomes more and more an adjunct of our spiritual life. In this regard, it is often helpful to determine what it is that we urgently need in order to take the next step on our spiritual path—and then invoke it. For some, this might be a greater knowledge of how spirit works. For others, it could be a need for a stronger rapport with spirit—or a new focus in serving the divine plan.

In many instances, the situations which inspire us to use the tool of invocation will involve other people. When this is the case, we can invoke assistance on their behalf as well as for ourself. In such situations, however, we must remember that we are not just invoking what is best for us, but what is best for all concerned. We must understand that there is a *collective need* which can be identified and defined from a spiritual perspective. It is this collective need which we must serve, if we are to be successful.

We might recognize, for example, that our family relationships are deficient in trust and love. Wanting to enrich the family environment, and make it more conducive to cooperation and growth, we invoke the divine forces of harmony and love on behalf of the entire family, not just ourself. We do not, however, then sit back and wait for God to strike. We change any attitudes and habits within ourself which might undermine the atmosphere of harmony and love—and we seize the opportunities which come to us to nurture and reinforce these qualities in other family members.

Just so, if work is a problem area because our boss has a number of irritating habits, we must rise above our personal need and focus instead on the collective need. This collective need would be what both of us should learn from this situation. Our boss may need to learn the right use of authority—but we need to learn the art of cooperation and a greater respect for authority. To work most successfully with invocation in a situation such as this, we need to invoke both qualities from the life of spirit and nurture them equally. If we do, we may be amazed by the way in which the lessons we learn inspire our boss to likewise learn.

One other excellent way of using invocation at the individual level is to summon inspiration and self-discipline to help us in our creative projects. Once again, however, it is important to realize that the scope of any genuine creative project is greater than just our personal need for success. If our creative work is to have any impact at all, it must meet the needs of those who will read it, watch it, listen to it, or in any way be touched by it. And so, the best way to use the tool of invocation for creative work is to invoke ideas, forces, and powers which will serve to enlighten and enrich human understanding, through our creative activity.

Invocation, of course, can also be used for the benefit of large groups—even the whole of humanity. In using invocation on a large scale, however, we must be especially careful to define the needs of the situation precisely and impersonally. All too often, we form opinions about what is best and right for humanity with an appalling lack of discernment. We let our prejudices rule us instead of looking at human conditions from the perspective of spirit; as a result, our opinions are highly colored by what is most convenient for us, serves our interests, or causes us the least distress.

It is commonplace, for example, for activist groups to believe that the problems which threaten them will only be solved when those who oppose them convert to their way of thinking—or at least give in to their point of view. It should be obvious that such attitudes are in no way harmonious with the life of spirit, however; their only aim is the elimination of symptoms, not the resolution of problems. Such groups can often rally great support, because they aim their appeal at the emotionalism and bigotry of the general public. But emotional militancy does not solve problems.

To invoke the life of spirit to help groups, nations, and the human race, we must examine the real issues involved with intelligence, discernment, and a thorough respect for the evolutionary designs and goals of spirit. Often, the first step is recognizing that both sides in any given situation have been guilty of provocation for a long, long time—and that both are lacking in tolerance, goodwill, fair play, and flexibility. In all too many human problems, each side expects the other to make all the changes; each side assumes that God and justice are on its side. But when this is the case, then no resolution is possible, until these attitudes are changed.

If we can understand this principle of human conflict in general, then it is easy to apply it to specific situations and to see the work which actually must be done. Whether it is the struggle between the Arab and Jewish worlds, between Irish Catholics and Protestants, among Hindus, Moslems, and Sikhs in India, or between blacks and whites, the full resolution of the conflict will not be easily attained. These conflicts are fueled by the momentum of century after century of struggle; until the combatants become thoroughly sick of their conflict and cry out to spirit for genuine help, they would only reject such help if it were offered.

But herein lies the clue for how to invoke resolution to these conflicts. The immediate need is not for peace, because peace cannot long endure where troublemakers are involved. The true need is for the troublemakers to come to realize the pointlessness and brutality of their actions and appreciate the value of goodwill in dealing with others. We know, of course, that these people cannot understand such subtleties—yet. But we can. So we dwell on the value of intelligent tolerance and compassion in dealing with others, and invoke it on their behalf. We review the usefulness of compromise and the sharing of authority, and invoke it on their behalf. We see the need for patience and nurturing the best within others, and invoke it on their behalf. As always, we must not be hypocritical; if we do not express these qualities in our own life, at least to some degree, we cannot invoke them for anyone else. (If that were the case, the first step to take would be to stop being a troublemaker ourself!) But if we are already an agent of these qualities and forces, we can work quite powerfully to invoke them for the good of mankind.

When we invoke the qualities and designs of the life of spirit for others, the power we invoke flows first to us. We must then radiate it to the group we are seeking to help. The actual steps of this kind of invocation are almost the same as with invocations for our own benefit; we define the true need, contact spirit in prayer or meditation, focus ourself at a mental level, direct our attention on calling forth the forces and qualities which will meet the need with enlightenment, and end with a blessing which radiates the force of spiritual assistance and power to the group we seek to help. Through the use of the creative imagination, we then envision the light of spiritual purpose and design enveloping the people in the group, to turn their hearts and minds toward spirit and absorb the qualities we have invoked. In this way, we create a channel for dispersing the light of our blessing.

Throughout this process, we must be sure to remember that we are invoking spiritual qualities—not specific objectives. Our role is to strengthen the maturity, wisdom, and goodwill of these people, so that they will begin to behave in more enlightened ways. Once we have said our invocation, we must leave the rest to the free will of the people in the group to reject or accept these qualities and forces, and initiate change on their own. More we cannot do!

Naturally, the work to help other groups is not something we have to do alone. It is possible to perform these invocations as part of a group of like-minded people. And this can have tremendous benefits, because a massed appeal can summon far greater force than the appeal of just one person. More importantly, when truly effective invocatory work is going to be done, the full force of spiritual powers to be invoked will often be so intense that it should not be borne by just one person. It takes a large number of people to transmit the great energies humanity needs for its evolution.

Group invocations need not be done only by those who gather together physically at one time and in one place, of course. Since the work of invocation is a mental process for summoning and directing spiritual energies, the work can be done by people scattered in many locations and acting at different times. The only requirement for effective group invocation is to share a common focus on the kind of divine energies to be summoned and a mutual respect for one another as agents of the divine plan for humanity. There must also be a capacity to rise above our personal focus. While it is quite satisfactory to invoke our own soul to help us solve our personal problems, we need to tap into more universal spiritual sources when working in group format on behalf of others. The most readily accessible sources of this kind are the Hierarchy and, occasionally, the angelic kingdom. The Hierarchy, headed by the Christ, is the inner and true government of world civilization and humanity. It is to the whole human race as our individual soul is to our personality. The Hierarchy is the custodian of the plan for the unfoldment of civilization and the divine potential of the human race, just as our soul is the custodian for our personal spiritual plan.

Obviously, as we become skilled in participating in genuine group invocations, we enter into wholly new reciprocal relationships. Our primary contact with spirit is still the soul, but as we broaden our duties as an agent of spirit, we likewise increase our understanding of spirit. Our skills as a spiritual person mature.

The Summons To Us

As we gain skill in the use of invocation, we ultimately come to realize that it is not just a fragment here and a facet there of the life of spirit that we invoke; to tap the full potential of this marvelous tool of spirit, we must see our role as invoking the whole fabric of spirit. At first, this may seem to be an impossible proposition, but the more we understand of spirit, the more it makes sense.

We begin to realize, for example, that the activities of our life are of little importance, unless we regard them in the context of contributing to the overall well-being and progress of civilization and humanity. In the rush to take care of pressing personal concerns, we often fail to observe how much we touch the lives of others. We need to respect the importance of the ordinary things we do—or fail to do.

Our contributions to life can be effective

even when they are not dramatic. Just being self-sufficient, economically and psychologically, so that we are a contributing member of society, is a way in which we enrich the life of humanity. Being a good worker, a compassionate parent, and a responsible citizen are all ways we add to the health of civilization—even though they are ordinary activities shared by many people.

In fact, this is part of the power of our life as a human being. We share most of our individual problems with millions of other people, just as we share most of our individual potential with millions of others. It is part of human nature to have problems—and to have talents and resources we can use to solve them. When we stop feeling sorry for ourself and cursing others for our problems, we can look at ourself and others in a new light. We are not alone in our frustrations—we have not been singled out for special humiliation or torture. And by the same token, the impact of our personal triumphs over adversity is not limited to ourself alone. As we strive to solve our problems intelligently, we lessen the burden of the whole human race. As we learn to identify our real needs for wisdom, patience, courage, goodwill, and joy, and call forth these qualities from the life of spirit, it is not we alone who benefit. All humanity is blessed by this inflow of divine force. We are actually adding it to the understanding and experience of all humanity, as well as our own. If we consciously recognize this aspect of invoking divine life, we can cooperate with it in many powerful ways.

With enough experience, we come to realize that we all draw our life from the same source. We share a common purpose and destiny. We are all governed by the authority of divine law. We therefore share a common heritage, a common duty, and a common burden. But if we share the work and the hardship, we also share the goal and reward of wholeness and perfection. And so it makes sense to view our life not just as an individual experience, but also as part of the collective experience of mankind.

As we understand more profoundly the role we play in mankind, we prepare ourself for *the real work of invocation—the opportunity to participate with God as a co-creator and preserver of life on earth.* Having trained ourself to respond to spiritual purpose through the use of invocation, we come to the point where we are able to truly serve as an agent of this plan in all we do—if we so choose. To do this, however, we must understand as much as we can about the work and destiny of the human race and the part we play in this drama. We must understand what humanity needs.

What does humanity need? Some would say fresh air and fresh water, but what we really need is a fresh approach to solving our problems—a more mental and rational focus. We need to rise out of the muck of our bigotry, nationalism, and competitive squabbling and learn to use goodwill as a basis for human and international relationships. We need a stronger ability to cooperate with others, expressing trust and generosity, rather than trying to create peace by maintaining a balance of destructive force.

There is an urgent need for developing the true creative potential of the mind and for using it to produce innovative approaches to society's problems. Instead of using the mind to rationalize old habits and selfish desires, we should be using it to discover and explore the higher realms of human and divine potential. Instead of using the mind to preserve and defend our prejudices and weaknesses, we should be using it to reveal and express the treasures of spirit—wisdom, joy, love, patience, steadfastness, and courage.

Instead of rushing to find our "roots" in an African jungle or a European ghetto, we should work to discover our roots in spirit—the roots which link us with all human beings, not just a limited few. We need to find and express the sense of unity and fellowship that is already alive and active at the level of the soul—and through it, learn to participate in the shared presence of the life of spirit. Only when we have found these roots will it become possible to rise above the petty conflicts which have historically divided us. Only then will we be able to generate the climate of trust, respect, and goodwill that is essential to solving humanity's problems.

The work of invocation teaches us something very important about our common ties with the rest of humanity, and its unbreakable bond with spirit. The most powerful invocations ever uttered on behalf of humanity have been the unspoken but clearly focused appeals of millions and millions of people who have recognized an urgent need and called out to spirit for help. At the time of the Civil War in America, for example, the United States faced a terrible crisis—the breakdown of the union which had held it together. With the nation divided on economic, political, and racial lines, it seemed as though it could not endure. Yet the invocatory appeal of the citizenry brought forth the person of Abraham Lincoln to preserve the union. In so doing, he added a new measure of humanitarian and charitable concern for the welfare of all citizens to our political life, thereby healing not only the old divisions which had split the nation but also the new wounds generated by the war itself. Similar crises brought forth the leadership of Franklin Delano Roosevelt and Sir Winston Churchill to lead the Western world through World War II.

As powerful as these massed appeals were, it is only at times of great crisis that people come together, even informally, to invoke this kind of help. And even then, it is a process which can backfire, because the invocation is usually vague and unfocused; it does not define the *specific* guidance, courage, and leadership which is needed. It should be kept in mind that at the time the United States called forth Roosevelt and England invoked Churchill, Germany provoked Adolph Hitler! The summons of the German masses apparently did not specify the quality of strong, effective leadership that was needed—and they called forth the wrong person.

To be an intelligent co-creator with God, we must constantly remember that the fabric of humanity is made up of people such as ourself. We cannot expect humanity to solve its problems unless we are involved in solving our own. Nor can we effectively participate in aligning the values, priorities, and goals of humanity with its spiritual design, unless we have done the same in our own life.

Invocation teaches us how to do this—and it also teaches us that we are constantly being evoked to make these changes. Our responsibility is therefore a dual one, consisting not only of invoking the qualities and forces mankind needs to take its next step on the spiritual path, but also of involving ourself in evoking or calling forth from the whole human race a stronger willingness to evolve.

The great example of evocation in this

regard is the raising of Lazarus from the dead by Jesus. Jesus was called to heal Lazarus, but arrived too late; Lazarus had already died and been entombed in a cave for several days. In one of the most shining examples of the work of the Christ, Jesus simply called for the mourners of Lazarus to be quiet and to roll the boulder away from the mouth of the tomb. Then, He called for Lazarus to come forth. And he did!

The Christ plays the same role as the great resurrecting force in our own life—and in the life of humanity. We often wait until it is almost too late to call for His help, and by the time the help arrives, we may have lost all hope. But the Christ calls for us to be quiet. In other words, we must quiet the doubting, skeptical, and anxious parts of our personality—or humanity as a whole—before the work of invocation can proceed. Our whole character must come together and generate a level of tension which summons new issues of spiritual life to us.

In raising Lazarus, the Christ then called for the boulder to the tomb to be removed. This is the removal of impediments which keep us from taking direct action to resolve our problems—a prejudice or bad habit individually, a long-standing tradition of hatred or bigotry at collective levels. Once the boulder of our blindness is rolled away, we can penetrate to the problem itself and work directly to meet its true need.

Jesus was quiet a moment, and then He spoke calmly to thank God for His constant love and support. Finally, He called for Lazarus to come forth from his cave. In many ways, the Christ spoke to all of us for all time at that moment. We, too, are summoned to come out of the cave of our limiting convictions, our materialistic vision, our self-indulgent focus, and our animosities and divisions. And as we respond to this summons, individually and collectively, we leave behind us the deadening weight of our unenlightened thinking. Our habits, individually, and our social traditions, collectively, are reborn at a new level of awareness and communion with the life of spirit.

Divine life evokes us, individually and collectively, even as we should learn to invoke divine life. In this way, we can arise from the dead like Lazarus and enter into a new life of active partnership with spirit. This is the promise of invocation.

A Complete Listing of the Essays in The Art of Living

Enriching the Personality
The Practice of Detachment
Finding Meaning in Life
Building Right Human Relationships
The Spirit of Generosity
Joy
Living Responsibly
The Nature and Purpose of the Emotions
Cultivating Tolerance and Forgiveness
Seeking Intelligent Guidance
The Bridge of Faith
Discerning Reality
Cooperating with Life
The Mind and Its Uses: Parts I and II
Coping with Stress
Enlightened Self-Discipline
Inspired Humility
The Act of Human Creation: Parts I & II
The Work of Patience
The Pursuit of Integrity
The Way to Health: Parts I and II
The Process of Self-Renewal
Filling Life with Beauty
Becoming Graceful
The Importance of Courage
The Noblest Masterpiece: Parts I and II

A Complete Listing of the Essays in The Life of Spirit

The Spiritual Person
The Spiritual Path
Defeating Evil and Sin
The Power of God: The Mother Aspect
The Power of God: The Son Aspect
The Power of God: The Father Aspect
The Treasures of Spirit
Redeeming Life
Psychic Dimensions of the Life of Spirit
The Role Death Plays in Life
The Trials of Initiation
The Path To Transfiguration
Praying Effectively
Enlightened Confession
The Act of Meditation
Invoking Divine Life
Worshipping God
Making Life Sacred
Finding Heaven on Earth
Linking Earth with Heaven
Harnessing Esoteric Traditions
The Inner Teachings of the Bible
Working with Angels
The Divine Workshop (7 essays)

Ordering Additional Essays

Other essays being issued in Enthea Press gift editions—the "Spiritual Companions" series—include *Working With Angels, Celebrating Life, The Act of Meditation, Healing Emotional Wounds, Defeating Evil and Sin, The Role Death Plays in Life, The Noble Mind & Its Uses, Finding Meaning in Life, The Light of Initiation, The Connection,* and *The Way To Health.* They may be ordered by emailing Enthea Press at lig201@lightariel.com or by sending a check plus shipping to Enthea Press, P.O. Box 251, Marble Hill, GA 30148.

Orders may also be paid with PayPal.

The rest of the essays are available only in their original form—as one of six essays in each volume of *The Art of Living* and *The Life of Spirit.* These books can be ordered for $18 apiece, plus $6 for shipping, $8 if ordering two or more books. The entire set of either *The Art of Living* or *The Life of Spirit* can be bought for $90 each, postpaid, or both series can be ordered together for $150. These books can be ordered from Enthea Press as well.

The Art of Living is also available in ebook format for $65.